Remodeling Kitchens

CREATIVE
PUBLISHING
international

MINNETONKA, MINNESOTA

Copyright © 1999
Creative Publishing international, Inc.
5900 Green Oak Drive
Minnetonka, Minnesota 55343
1-800-328-3895
All rights reserved
Printed in U.S.A.

Books available in this series:
*Everyday Home Repairs, Decorating With
Paint & Wallcovering, Carpentry: Tools •
Shelves • Walls • Doors, Building Decks,
Home Plumbing Projects & Repairs, Basic
Wiring & Electrical Repairs, Workshop Tips
& Techniques, Advanced Home Wiring,
Carpentry: Remodeling, Landscape
Design & Construction, Bathroom
Remodeling, Built-in Projects for the Home,
Refinishing & Finishing Wood, Exterior
Home Repairs & Improvements, Home
Masonry Repairs & Projects, Building
Porches & Patios, Flooring Projects &
Techniques, Advanced Deck Building,
Advanced Home Plumbing*

Library of Congress
Cataloging-in-Publication Data

Remodeling kitchens.

p. cm. -- (Black & Decker home
improvement library)
Includes index.
ISBN   0-86573-638-3 (softcover)
1. Kitchens--Remodeling--Amateurs'
manuals. I. Creative Publishing International. II. Series.
TH4816.3.K58R46   1999
643' .4--dc21   98-49173

President/CEO: David D. Murphy
Vice President/Editorial: Patricia K. Jacobsen
Vice President/Retail Sales & Marketing:
 Richard M. Miller

REMODELING KITCHENS
Created by: The Editors of Creative Publishing
international, Inc., in cooperation with Black &
Decker. ● **BLACK&DECKER** is a trademark of the
Black & Decker Corporation and is used under
license.

Contents

Introduction. **4**

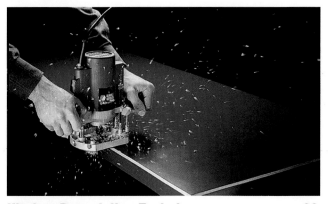

Kitchen Remodeling Techniques. **29**

Flooring. **62**

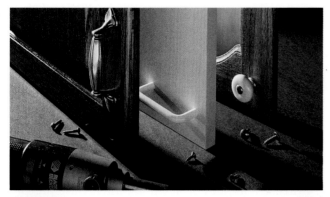

Executive Editor: Bryan Trandem
Associate Creative Director: Tim Himsel
Managing Editor: Jennifer Caliandro

Project Manager: Michelle Skudlarek
Editor: Paul Currie
Senior Art Director: Kevin Walton
Copy Editor: Janice Cauley
Illustrator: Jon Simpson
Mac Production Artist: Joe Fahey

Vice President of Photography & Production: Jim Bindas
Manager, Production Services: Kim Gerber
Production Manager: Stasia Dorn
Shop Supervisor: Dan Widerski
Studio Services Manager: Marcia Chambers
Studio Services Coordinator: Carol Osterhus
Photo Team Leader: Chuck Nields
Photographers: Tate Carlson, Andrea Rugg

Contributing Manufacturers: American Brush Company, Inc.; American Olean Tile Co.; American Woodmark Corp.; Architext; Armstrong World Industries, Inc.; Bruce Hardwood Floors; Cooper Industries (in-cluding registered trademarks: Crescent, Lufkin, Nicholson, Plumb, Turner, Weller, Wire-Wrap, Wiss, Xcelite); Crystal Cabinets; Dap, Inc.; Harris-Tarkett Inc.; H.B. Fuller Co.; In-Sink-Erator; Jenn-Air Co.; Roth Distributing; Sandvik Saws & Tools Co.; The Stanley Works; United Gilsonite Lab-oratories; USG Corp.; V.T. Industries; Wilsonart/Ralph Wilson Plastics Co.

Printed on American paper by:
R. R. Donnelley & Sons Co.
10 9 8 7 6 5 4

Introduction

Every home needs a beautiful and well-planned kitchen. But the idea of remodeling can be intimidating, considering the many decisions that need to be made, and the number of building techniques required. *Remodeling Kitchens* contains all the information needed to successfully make your kitchen into the attractive and functional room your household deserves. From practical advice about design to professional building techniques you can do, you will find everything you need. And you will save a great deal of money by making wise decisions and doing some or most of the work yourself.

The first section of the book shows you how to design and plan a kitchen remodeling project. First, you'll find out how to evaluate what level of remodeling project you require. This can range from a simple facelift with repainted cabinets and new flooring, to a complete demolition and renovation.

Then, you'll learn how to determine the specific needs your new kitchen space must meet, including the standards that professional kitchen designers use to ensure that kitchen components are well placed and comfortable for working. You'll also see how to draw plans that will help you obtain the necessary building permits, as well as guide your building efforts.

The second section of the book contains step-by-step instructions for all building techniques specifically required in a kitchen remodeling project: installing plumbing, wiring, flooring, cabinets, countertops, fixtures, and appliances. If you aren't familiar with the basic tool and material techniques for each of these areas, see the appropriate volumes in our Black & Decker Home Improvement Library™: *Carpentry: Remodeling, Advanced Home Wiring, Advanced Home Plumbing,* and *Flooring Projects & Techniques.*

First, we'll introduce you to the basic hand and power tools you'll need to complete your new kitchen, including the plumbing and wiring. Some of these tools you may already own, since they're common to many home improvement projects. But you'll also learn about some specialty tools you'll need to rent to accomplish certain remodeling tasks.

Then, you'll learn the essentials of plumbing a remodeled kitchen. You'll see how to run new water supply and drain-waste-vent pipes, and how to run plumbing pipes to an island sink.

The modern kitchen is a home's greatest consumer of electrical power. In the next section, you'll see how to meet those powerful demands by adding new circuits. Information about providing adequate task lighting in the kitchen is also given.

After plumbing and wiring, you'll learn how to install underlayment and flooring. Learn how to work with resilient sheet vinyl, vinyl tiles, hardwood strips and planks, plastic laminated flooring, and ceramic tile.

In the cabinet chapter, you'll discover how to improve existing cabinets with paint, or how to remove and replace all your kitchen cabinets.

For countertops, you'll see instructions on installing post-form laminate countertops, and making and installing your own plastic laminate or ceramic tile countertops.

Finally, we'll show you how to install and hook up the fixtures and appliances in your new kitchen. All major appliances are shown, from faucets and dishwashers to water filtration systems.

Remodeling Kitchens is the complete guide you need to efficiently and cost-effectively improve your home. Whether your kitchen needs a fresh style change or a completely new layout and expansion, the information in this book will help you achieve the kitchen of your dreams.

A well-designed kitchen serves as the center of activities in the home. Plenty of storage space and work areas make it well equipped to be an efficient food preparation area. Open countertops and serving areas that don't obstruct traffic patterns provide comfortable places to talk over coffee, eat together, or do household paperwork. And design elements like wood or tile floors, polished granite countertops, copper vent hoods, and glass-fronted cabinets make the kitchen a beautiful place in which to visit or work.

Kitchen Planning

Interior Woodstains

TRADITIONAL COLORS

OAK

PINE

OAK

INTERIOR
#8310 CON
#8410 WATE

7 - ANTI

1 - NA

1 -

2 - LIGHT O

No. R590-18 WESTCOTT® Flexible Stainless

BREAKFAST
TABLE

BREAKFA
7'6X10'0

KITCHEN
0X11'6

RANGE

4'-3"

DINING
12'6X10'6

NE

Determining Your Needs

If your kitchen is worth remodeling, it's only logical that you take the time and effort to make sure the finished project will meet your great expectations. The annals of home remodeling are filled with tales of rushed and ill-advised kitchen remodeling projects that ended with homeowners who were both disappointed and impoverished.

A crucial first step toward your future satisfaction is to carefully evaluate your present kitchen and determine what problems it has and what features are lacking. Creating a new kitchen that simply puts a new face on old problems may make you feel better for the moment, but it's ultimately a waste of time—and an expensive waste of time, at that. If you take the time now to determine what features are necessary and appropriate for your new kitchen, this effort will pay big dividends in the end.

Your motives for remodeling your kitchen probably fall into one of two categories: solving functional problems, or improving the room's aesthetic appearance. In other words, either your kitchen is inconvenient for your family to use, or you just can't stand the way it looks. Or maybe it's both dysfunctional and ugly. A logical place to begin, then, is by documenting the elements that need improvement.

Getting Started

Begin by simply taking a week or two to observe how you now use your kitchen. Keep a note pad handy and jot down any major or minor problems and annoyances that prevent you from being as efficient or comfortable as you'd like to be when cooking or eating. Also note those elements of the room that are just plain unattractive. Books and magazines on kitchen design and decorating can help you identify problem elements.

Once you have documented the problems with your kitchen, give your imagination permission to roam. Don't worry about money yet. This is your dream kitchen, after all, and there will be plenty of time to bring your fantasies down to earth as you begin the hard planning stages. Now is the time to consider every possibility. We know one family, for example, who were so fond of entertaining in the kitchen that they installed a large-screen television and fireplace. Another couple made room in their kitchen space for an elaborate home fitness center. Your secret fantasy might be as simple as installing pantry shelves in your cabinets, or as major as installing a glassed-in garden sun-room off the kitchen.

If you've lived with a small kitchen for many years, you may think of it as simply a work space in which to prepare meals, clean up dishes, and store foods and utensils. As you brainstorm for kitchen ideas, remember that this room can serve many more functions, as well. If your kitchen has no eating area, consider changing the layout to add a cozy breakfast nook. If your home doesn't have a den or study, think about including a home office and study desk in your new kitchen.

If you find it difficult to create a mind's-eye vision of your new kitchen, then look for ideas studying the kitchens in other people's homes. Model home shows sponsored by builders also are good places to look for inspiration, and kitchen design magazines can also help.

Finally, consider how your kitchen will be used over the next five to twenty years. The needs of a family with young children soon to become active, boisterous teenagers are much different than the needs of a mature family whose children are about to leave the nest for college.

For convenience, we've grouped the various elements of a kitchen into six (see box) categories to help you when determining your needs. As you evaluate your current kitchen and plan your new space, use a sheet of paper and make a checklist to record your decisions. You'll be able to refer to this checklist as you continue to plan your project.

Basic Layout & Floor Plan

Level 1: The cosmetic makeover. Though relatively inexpensive, this option can be enormously rewarding. While retaining the same basic layout of the kitchen, you replace the flooring and, in some cases, the countertops. You'll also be repainting or installing new wallpaper, and may want to install new storage features in your cabinets. Appliances and fixtures are usually retained, unless their age and condition make replacement necessary. DIY cost: $1,000 to $7,000.

Does your present kitchen area provide adequate room for working and eating? Are the traffic patterns convenient? If traffic movement between doors crosses the room diagonally, you may find it difficult to work, since other family members are constantly crossing your path. Does your kitchen have an adequate eating area? Does the location of the eating area interrupt traffic or interfere with your ability to work in the kitchen?

Sometimes these problems can be corrected by a relatively simple rearrangement within the existing kitchen space, but in more serious cases, you may need to consider adding or moving doorways or expanding the size of the kitchen.

Kitchen remodeling projects can be categorized according to how much change is made to the layout and floor plan of the room, as illustrated on the next page. If virtually no changes are made to the layout and floor plan, you may get by with a Level 1 project—a relatively simple cosmetic makeover. This kind of makeover often appeals to homeowners planning to do much or all of the work themselves. Level 2 and Level 3 kitchens, which involve moderately complex changes to the layout, appeal to homeowners who may feel more comfortable sharing the work with a remodeling professional. Level 4 and Level 5 projects involve major changes to the floor plan and will require substantial help from remodeling professionals—unless you are an extremely experienced and successful do-it-yourselfer.

Level 2: Changing the layout:

With this option, you'll retain the same basic floor space as the existing kitchen, but will change the positions of the appliances, fixtures, and eating areas to create a more efficient floor plan. This level of remodeling includes most elements of the cosmetic makeover, but may also require the work of a carpenter, electrician, and plumber. Homeowners with ample do-it-yourself experience might choose to do most of this work themselves. DIY cost: $3,000 to $10,000.

Level 3: Redirecting traffic:

In a slightly more complicated scenario, you might find it necessary to change the layout more radically in order to redirect traffic moving through the kitchen. Often this means adding or moving a doorway in a partition wall, as well as redesigning the basic kitchen layout. Unless you are a very experienced do-it-yourselfer, much of this work will require the help of a carpenter and other subcontractors. At this fairly extensive level of remodeling, many homeowners also take the opportunity to add new windows, patio doors, and skylights. DIY cost: $6,000 to $30,000.

Level 4: Expanding inward:

If your present kitchen just isn't large enough to accommodate your needs, one option is to extend the space by borrowing space from adjacent rooms. This generally means that interior partition walls will need to be removed or moved, which is work for an experienced home construction carpenter. This level of remodeling often includes significant rearrangement of the appliances and cabinets, as well as the installation of new windows, doors, or skylights. In a major remodeling project of this kind, some homeowners may want to hire professional contractors for some of the work. DIY cost: $25,000 to $60,000.

Level 5: Expanding outward:

This is the Cadillac of kitchen remodeling possibilities, as big as it gets. If you find more space essential and can't expand inward into adjoining rooms, then the last option is to build an addition onto your home. This ambitious undertaking requires the aid of virtually the same collection of professionals it takes to build a home from scratch: architects and engineers, excavation and concrete contractors, construction and finish carpenters, plumbers and electricians. At this level, some homeowners choose to hire a general contractor to manage the project. Typical cost: $40,000 and up.

Countertops & Work Areas

Because a kitchen is first and foremost a space for preparing meals, nearly every kitchen is improved by increasing the countertop space. Does your kitchen have adequate space for performing all kitchen tasks? If two or more people work in the kitchen at the same time, are you able to work efficiently without bumping into one another? Is there adequate countertop work space around the sink, cooktop, oven, and refrigerator? Do you have at least one long, uninterrupted countertop for assembling meals and preparing complicated recipes? Or perhaps you have the more unusual problem of too much space, with the sink, stove, and refrigerator too far apart to be convenient.

If your goal in remodeling the kitchen is simply to improve the real estate value of your home in preparation for selling it, there are some special considerations for you.

In general, real estate agents say that investing in a luxury kitchen isn't a great idea if you plan to sell in the near future, since it will be difficult to recoup the money you spend on top-of-the-line appliances, cabinets, and countertops. Instead, make sure the basic kitchen layout is sound, and replace aging materials with good-quality, medium-price products.

Rather than installing an integral solid-surface sink and countertop, for example, go with a stainless steel sink and laminate countertop. Instead of pricey ceramic tile or solid hardwood floors, go with a good-quality vinyl sheet flooring.

Planned wisely, a remodeled kitchen can pay for itself in home equity, but remember that real estate values vary widely depending on neighborhood and economic conditions. It's a good idea to consult with a good real estate agent, who can tell you how much a remodeled kitchen is actually worth in your situation.

These problems can sometimes be remedied with a Level 2 or Level 3 kitchen rearrangement, but if you clearly don't have enough working space, the most effective solution may be to expand the physical size of the kitchen with a Level 4 or Level 5 kitchen expansion.

Sometimes the problem is not lack of countertops, but simply lack of clear space. Do small appliances, such as toasters or microwave ovens, take up valuable countertop space in your kitchen? If so, the solution may be to install specialty cabinets to store these items and free up your countertops. Do you need space for working on household paperwork? If so, consider revising the kitchen layout to include a home office area.

Even if your work areas provide adequate space, it's possible the countertops are just plain worn or unattractive. Countertops are one of the main visual elements of the kitchen, and replacing them is common, even in simple cosmetic remodeling projects.

Countertops must be both functional and attractive. Plan for enough usable work space and choose a material that suits your decorating scheme. Keep in mind what kind of care the countertop material requires.

Cabinets & Storage

Adding or replacing cabinets is one of the most common goals in a kitchen remodeling project. Does your kitchen have adequate storage space for food, dishes, and utensils? Are kitchen items stored near their point of use? In other words, are dishes stored near the dishwasher, and dry packaged foods near the cooktop and oven? Are the items used most frequently stored so they are 2½ to 5 ft. above the floor?

These problems sometimes can be addressed by simple reorganization of the existing cabinets, or by adding cabinet organizer features, such as pantry doors and slide-out shelves. And make sure you're making good use of all possible spaces, including corners and the spaces above appliances.

Sometimes, however, the only logical option will be to change the kitchen layout or expand the space to include more storage cabinets. In rarer situations, you may have more cabinet space than you need. If so, you can consider converting some of this storage space into a countertop eating area, or to an additional appliance, such as a trash compactor.

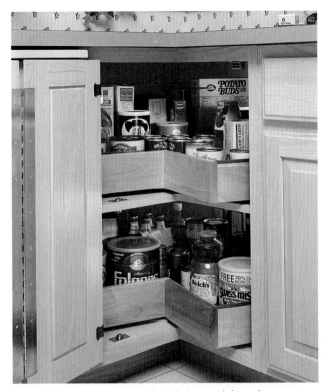

Lack of storage space is a big problem in many kitchens. In this remodeling project, the homeowners installed a Lazy Susan designed to reclaim valuable space in a previously hard-to-reach area.

Power & Lighting

Do you blow fuses or trip circuit breakers whenever the toaster and electric skillet are operating together? If your kitchen is typical, it probably doesn't have enough electrical circuits to power the increasing number of electrical appliances used in the modern kitchen. In all likelihood, you'll want to add more circuits when you remodel.

Is your kitchen too dark overall? This problem can be remedied by adding overhead light fixtures or by installing skylights or additional windows. Is there adequate task lighting at each work area, or do you find yourself squinting nervously when chopping produce with a sharp knife? Adding ceiling track lights or under-cabinet light fixtures will make your kitchen a safer and more comfortable place to work.

Simply replacing unattractive old lighting fixtures with new fixtures can dramatically improve the appearance of your kitchen. In most cases, this kind of replacement requires no extensive rewiring.

A well-planned kitchen will have good overall lighting, adequate task lighting on work areas, and accent lighting to highlight decorative features of the room.

Appliances & Plumbing Fixtures

Evaluate your appliances and plumbing fixtures. Most appliances and plumbing faucets more than 15 years old are nearing the ends of their useful lives, and probably should be replaced when you remodel the kitchen. In addition, modern energy-efficient appliances can actually save you money over the long run.

Many homeowners replace plumbing fixtures and appliances simply for cosmetic reasons. But before you discard a good-quality, well-running appliance for this reason, investigate the possibility of refacing it to match your new decorating scheme.

Is your present microwave oven a newer, built-in model? If not, consider replacing it with a microwave that slides into a dedicated cabinet. Is your sink in good shape and adequate for your needs? Adding a second utility sink is increasingly popular in big kitchen remodeling projects.

In addition to the standard kitchen appliances, take a look at the variety of clever and useful small appliances and accessories now available. These include trash compactors, warming drawers, water purifiers, instant-hot-water taps, cabinet-mounted can openers, and built-in stereo and television units.

Some appliances can be finished with wood panels that match the rest of the kitchen cabinetry. This creates a more unified look for the kitchen.

Floors, Walls & Ceilings

Floors, walls, and ceilings are the important visual elements in a kitchen, providing a backdrop for the cabinets and countertops. In a cosmetic makeover, changing these elements alone can create an entirely new feel in your kitchen.

The flooring is usually replaced during a remodeling project—even in simple cosmetic makeovers. If you have a hardwood or ceramic tile floor in good condition, however, it is possible to clean and refinish the surface. Similarly, wall surfaces are generally renewed during any remodeling project. In a cosmetic makeover, this may involve simply repainting or hanging new wallpaper. If your project involves wall construction, or if the wall surfaces are in poor condition, you will need to install new drywall or plaster. Other options include installing wood paneling, wall coverings, or decorative metal ceiling panels.

Ceramic tile offers excellent durability and can create boldly patterned floors.

Creating Plans

Once you have a good idea of the features you want in your new kitchen, it's time to create detailed plan drawings. Good plan drawings will help you in several phases of the planning process:

• Selecting cabinets and appliances to fit your kitchen layout.

• Soliciting accurate work bids when negotiating with plumbers, electricians, and other subcontractors.

• Obtaining a building permit at your local Building Inspections office.

• Scheduling the stages of a remodeling project.

• Evaluating the work of contractors. If a carpenter or cabinetmaker fails to meet your expectations, your plan drawings serve as proof that the contractor did not complete the work as agreed.

Codes & Standards

Creating plans for a kitchen can seem like an overwhelming challenge, but fortunately there are guidelines available to help you. Some of these guidelines are legal regulations specified by your local Building Code and must be followed exactly. Most codes have very specific rules for basic construction, as well as for plumbing and electrical installations.

Another set of guidelines, known as standards, are informal recommendations developed over time by kitchen designers, cabinetmakers, and appliance manufacturers. These design standards suggest parameters for good kitchen layout, and following them helps ensure that your kitchen is comfortable and convenient to use.

Guidelines for Layout

The goal of any kitchen layout is to make the cook's work easier and, where possible, to allow other people to enjoy the same space without getting in the way. Understanding the accepted design standards can help you determine whether your present layout is sufficient or if your kitchen needs a more radical layout change or expansion.

Work triangle & traffic patterns. A classic kitchen design concept, the work triangle theory proposes that the sink, range, and refrigerator be arranged in a triangular layout according to the following guidelines:

• Position of the triangle should be such that traffic flow will not disrupt the main functions of the kitchen.

• Total distance between the corners of the triangle should be no more than 26 ft. and no less than 12 ft.

The work triangle is a layout concept that lets you develop a convenient arrangement of the range, sink, and refrigerator in the kitchen.

• Each side of the triangle should be between 4 and 9 ft. in length.

If two people frequently work in the kitchen simultaneously, the layout should include two work triangles. In a two-triangle kitchen, the triangles may share one side, but they should not cross one another.

Don't fret too much if you can't make the triangle layout work perfectly. Some kitchens, for example, may have four work stations instead of three, and others may not have enough space to accommodate the classic triangle.

For general traffic design, it is recommended to leave 4-ft. "corridors" between all stationary items for walking comfort. Some designers will allow this standard to be reduced to 3 ft. in smaller kitchens.

Countertop space. Lack of kitchen countertop space is one of the biggest complaints heard from homeowners and, in some cases, is the primary reason for remodeling the kitchen. Tables 1 and 2 on page 32 outline the minimum standards for countertop space. Also make sure your kitchen has at least one food preparation area with an uninterrupted length of countertop that is at least 36" long.

Appliances. Table 1 shows standard dimensions for common kitchen appliances—information you can use when planning your layout. These dimensions are standard from manufacturer to manufacturer, although larger and smaller models may also be available.

Some things to keep in mind when planning the location of appliances in your kitchen layout:

• *Appliance* doors should open away from traffic areas and other appliances.

• *Proper spacing* around appliances is crucial. Leave an open space at least 30" × 48" in front of each appliance.

Cabinets. Table 2 on page 18 shows the minimum standards for cabinet storage in small and large kitchens. The blind, unusable portion of a corner cabinet should not be included when calculating linear footage for either wall or base cabinets.

The sizes of base cabinets and wall cabinets are fairly uniform among manufacturers, and unless you have them custom-built in unusual sizes, they will conform to the following standards:

• Base cabinets: height—34½"; depth—23" to 24"; width—9" to 48", in 3" increments.

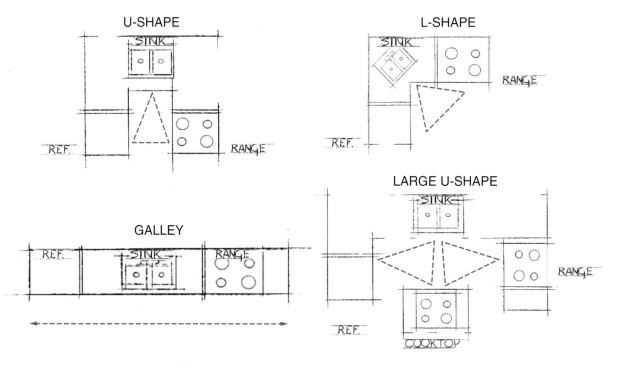

Some common kitchen arrangements include the U-shape, L-shape, and corridor (galley) kitchen. Larger L- and U-shaped kitchens can often accommodate an island cabinet, which can shorten the legs of the kitchen triangle and make the cook's work easier.

- **Wall cabinets:** height—12", 15", 18", 24", 30", 33", 42"; depth—12"; width—24", 30", 33", 36", 42", 48".

- **Oven cabinets:** height—84", 96"; depth—24"; width—27", 30", 33".

- **Utility cabinets:** height—84"; depth—12", 24"; width—18", 24", 36".

Not every manufacturer will offer all these sizes and styles, so it's a good idea to obtain product catalogs when planning the layout of cabinets. Some other tips:

- *Use functional corner cabinets* rather than "blind" cabinets that provide no access to the corner area.

- *Include at least five storage/organizing units,* such as swing-out pantry units, appliance garages, and specialized drawers or shelves.

Eating areas. Kitchen tabletops and countertops used for dining are generally positioned 30", 36", or 42" above the floor, and the recommended space for each person varies according to the height of the surface. Table 3 on page 18 shows the recommended per-person clearances for eating areas.

Islands. A kitchen island should be positioned so there is at least 36" of clear space between the edges of its countertop and surrounding walls or cabinets.

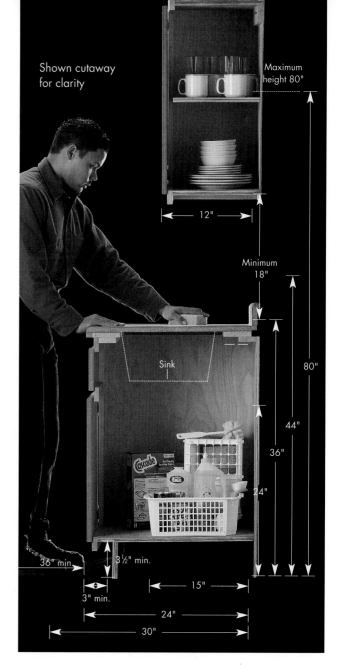

Shown cutaway for clarity

Table 1: Appliance Dimensions & Countertop Allowance

Appliance	Standard Dimension	Minimum Countertop Space	Comments
Refrigerator	36"	18" on latch side	12 cu. ft. for family of four; 2 cu. ft. for each additional
Sink	27" single 36" double	24" on one side 18" on other side	Minimum of 3" of countertop space between sink and edge of base cabinet
Range	36"	15" on one side 9" on other side	If a window is positioned above a cooking appliance, the bottom edge of the window casing must be at least 24" above the cooking surface
Cooktop	36"	15" on one side 9" on other side	
Wall oven	30"	15" on either side	Bottom edge should be between 24" and 48" above the floor
Microwave	24"	15" on either side	

Table 2: Cabinet Standards

Recommended Minimums	Kitchen Size	
	Less than 150 sq. ft.	More than 150 sq. ft.
Countertops	132 lin."	198 lin."
Base cabinets	156 lin."	192 lin."
Wall cabinets	144 lin."	186 lin."
Roll-out shelving	120 lin."	165 lin."

Table 3: Eating Surface Standards

	Height of Eating Surface		
	30"	36"	42"
Min. width for each seated diner	30"	24"	24"
Min. depth for each seated diner	19"	15"	12"
Minimum knee space	19"	15"	12"

Tables 1, 2, and 3 give recommended minimum spacing standards set by the National Kitchen & Bath Association. Following these guidelines helps ensure maximum convenience.

Guidelines for Basic Construction

If you are planning a major remodeling project that involves moving or adding walls, or building a new room addition, your plans must accurately show the locations and dimensions of the new walls and all doors and windows. This will allow the construction carpenter to give you an accurate bid on the work and will allow him to obtain the necessary building permits.

Windows. Most Building Codes require that kitchens have at least one window, with at least 10 sq. ft. of glass area. Some local Building Codes, however, will allow windowless kitchens, so long as they have proper venting. Kitchen designers recommend that kitchens have windows, doors, or skylights that together have a total glass surface area equal to at least 25% of the total floor area.

Doors. Exterior entry doors should be at least 3 ft. wide and 6½ ft. high. Interior passage doors between rooms must be at least 2½ ft. wide. A kitchen must have at least two points of entry, arranged so traffic patterns don't intrude on work areas.

Adding windows, doors, or skylights, or moving walls, can involve major structural work. Your plan drawings should show the location and dimensions of all windows and doors in your new kitchen.

Guidelines for Electrical Service & Lighting

Examine your circuit breaker panel, usually located in the basement of your home or in an attached garage. It may have an index that identifies circuits serving the kitchen. If your service panel has open slots, an electrician can add additional kitchen circuits relatively easily. If your service panel is full, he may have to install a new service panel at additional cost.

Nearly any kitchen remodeling project will require some upgrading of the electrical service. While your old kitchen may be served by a single 120-volt circuit, it's not uncommon for a large modern kitchen to require as many as seven individual circuits. And in a few cases, the extra demands of the new kitchen may require that the main electrical service for your entire house be upgraded by an electrician. By comparing the electrical service in your present kitchen with the requirements described below, you'll get an idea of how extensive your electrical service improvements will need to be. Your plan drawings should indicate the locations of all the outlets, lighting fixtures, and electrical appliances in your new kitchen.

The National Electric Code requires the following for kitchens:

• *Two small-appliance circuits* (120-volt, 20-amp) to supply power for the refrigerator and plug-in countertop appliances.

• *Wall outlets* spaced no more than 12 ft. apart.

• *Countertop outlets* spaced no more than 4 ft. apart.

• *GFCI* (ground-fault circuit interrupter), protected receptacles installed in any general use outlet,

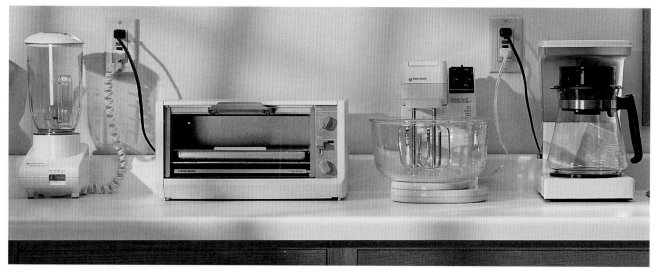

Kitchens have many electrical appliances, so make sure your remodeled kitchen has enough outlets. Code requires that outlets be spaced no more than 4 ft. apart behind countertops, but many kitchen designers space them even closer together. All outlets should have GFCI receptacles to reduce the possibility of shock.

whether above counter or at floor level.

• *Dedicated circuits* for each major appliance. Install a 20-amp, 120-volt circuit for a built-in microwave, a 15-amp circuit for the dishwasher and food disposer. An electrical range, cooktop, or wall oven requires a dedicated 50-amp, 240-volt circuit.

The Electrical Code only requires that a kitchen have some form of lighting controlled by a wall switch, but kitchen designers have additional recommendations:

• *A general lighting circuit* (120-volt, 15-amp) that operates independently from plug-in outlets.

• *Plentiful task lighting,* usually mounted under wall cabinets or soffits, to illuminate each work area.

• *Decorative lighting fixtures* to highlight attractive cabinets or other features of the kitchen.

Plentiful lighting makes your kitchen an appealing and comfortable place to work. A kitchen should have general overhead lighting, controlled by a wall switch, and well-lighted work areas, illuminated either by recessed canister light fixtures or under-cabinet fixtures.

Guidelines for Plumbing

If your new kitchen layout changes the location of the sink, or if you are planning to add an additional sink or dishwasher, the water supply and drain pipes will need to be upgraded. Your plan drawings should indicate these intended changes.

Extending plumbing lines for a new kitchen is often fairly easy and surprisingly inexpensive, but there are some exceptions you should note:

Old pipes. If your present plumbing is more than 25 years old, there is a good chance the plumber will recommend replacing these pipes before installing the kitchen fixtures. Depending on circumstances, this can be an expensive proposition, but if you're faced with this decision, we strongly urge you to take a deep breath and do what the plumber suggests. Those corroded old pipes will need to be replaced someday, and this work is easier and cheaper if you're already in the process of remodeling the kitchen.

Outdated systems. Older plumbing systems may have drain trap and vent arrangements that violate modern Code requirements. If your plumber needs to run all-new vent pipes, this will probably increase his fee.

Island sinks. If your new kitchen will include an island sink, your plumber will need to run vent pipes beneath the floor. For this reason, plumbing an island sink is more expensive than plumbing a wall sink.

Guidelines for Heating, Ventilation & Air-conditioning

Your plan drawings should also show the locations of heating/air-conditioning registers or fixtures in your proposed kitchen. If you're planning a cosmetic make-over or a simple layout change, there is a pretty good chance you can get by with the same registers, radiators, or heaters found in your present kitchen. But if your new kitchen will be substantially larger than it is now, or if the ratio of wall space filled by glass windows and doors will be greater, it's possible that you'll need to expand its heating/cooling capacity.

Increasing your kitchen's heating and cooling

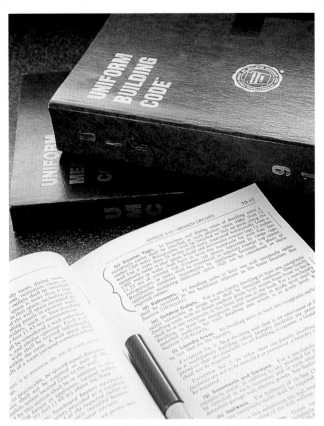

Code books can help you understand the structural, electrical, and plumbing requirements for kitchens. In addition to the formal Code books, which are written for professional tradesmen, there are many Code handbooks available that are written for homeowners. Bookstores and libraries carry both the formal Code books and Code handbooks.

can be as simple as extending ducts by a few feet, or as complicated as installing a new furnace. When installing a large room addition, for instance, you may learn that the present furnace is too small to adequately heat the now-increased floor space of your home.

How do you determine what your kitchen needs in the way of expanded heating and cooling? Unless you happen to be a mechanical engineer, you'll need to consult a professional to evaluate your heating/ventilation/air-conditioning (HVAC) system. The Code requirements for room heating are quite simple, but the methods used to calculate required energy needs of a room are fairly complex.

The Building Code requires simply that a room must be able to sustain a temperature of 70°F, measured at a point 3 ft. above the floor. When you contact an HVAC contractor, he'll use a complicated formula to calculate the most effi-

Vent hoods are required by Code on all ranges and cooktops. The vent fan exhausts cooking fumes and moisture to the outdoors.

cient way to meet this Code requirement. You can make his job easier by knowing the following information:

• *The exact dimensions of your kitchen.*

• *The thickness and amount of insulation* in the walls.

• *The number of doors and windows,* including their size and their energy ratings.

• *The total square footage of your house.*

• *The heating and cooling capacity* of your furnace and central air-conditioner, measured in BTUs. This information, usually printed on the

unit's access panel, will help the HVAC contractor determine if the system can adequately serve your new kitchen.

Finally, your cooktop should be equipped with an electric vent hood to exhaust cooking fumes and moisture from the kitchen. The volume of air moved by a vent fan is restricted by Code, so you should always check with a Building Inspector before selecting a vent hood.

Metal ductwork for the vent hood must be run through an exterior wall or through the ceiling. If your cooktop is located in an island cabinet, the ductwork must be routed through the floor, making for a more complicated and expensive installation.

Drawing Plans

Now the fun starts. Armed with a vision of the features you want to include in your new kitchen and equipped with an understanding of the Code requirements and design standards, you're ready to put pencil to paper and begin to develop plan drawings—the next important step in transforming your dream kitchen into reality.

The key to success when developing plan drawings is to take as much time as you need and to remain flexible. A professional kitchen designer might take 30 to 80 hours to come up with precise floor plans and elevation drawings, so it's not unreasonable to allow yourself several weeks if you're doing this work yourself. You will almost certainly revise your plans several times before you settle on a layout that feels right to you. And it's not uncommon for kitchen plans to undergo changes as you make decisions about appliances and other materials. As you begin to research the price of cabinets and appliances and receive bids from contractors, you may well decide that it's prudent to scale back for the sake of your bank account, and these changes may require you to revise your plan drawings.

Pages 26 to 27 provide the symbols commonly used to indicate kitchen features. Use these with graph paper to draw plans. We recommend that you photocopy these pages or use scratch paper for your first tries, reserving the printed pages for your finished drawings.

Developed plans for a kitchen remodeling project should include both floor plans and elevation drawings.

Finished plans for a kitchen remodeling project should include a scaled floor plan—a scale drawing made from an overhead perspective, showing exact room dimensions, as well as the location of windows, doors, cabinets, and appliances.

How to Create Floor Plans & Elevation Drawings

A floor plan (photo, above) is a scaled drawing made from an overhead perspective, showing the exact room dimensions, as well as the location of windows, doors, cabinets, appliances, electrical and plumbing fixtures. Elevation drawings are plans depicting a wall surface as if viewed from the side. For clarity, use the symbols provided on pages 26 to 27 to show the position of appliances and fixtures in your kitchen plans. Carpenters, electricians, plumbers, and other contractors will understand exactly what you want if your plan drawings speak their language.

The process of creating finished plans for a kitchen project takes time and is done in three phases. First, you'll be drawing a floor plan of your present kitchen, providing a reference on which to base your new design. Next, you'll be experimenting with various layout options to find a design that best suits your needs, a process that can take several days, or even weeks. Finally, you'll be creating precise, finished floor plans and elevation drawings, which you will use when you begin interviewing contractors to do the work.

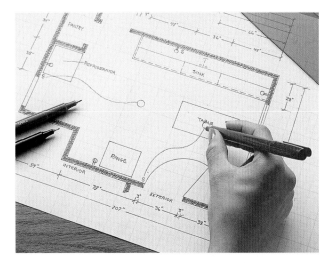

1 Measure each wall in your kitchen as it now exists. Take accurate measurements of the position and size of every feature, including doors, windows, cabinets, countertops, and appliances. Also note the locations of all light fixtures and electrical outlets. Using graph paper, create a scaled floor plan of your present kitchen, using a scale of ½" equals 1 ft. (If necessary, you can tape two or more sheets of graph paper together.) Indicate doors, windows, interior and exterior walls. Add the remaining elements, including the cabinets, appliances, and countertops, electrical outlets and lights, plumbing fixtures, and HVAC registers and fixtures. In the margins, mark the exact dimensions of all elements of the kitchen.

2 Using tracing paper overlayed on your kitchen drawing, begin sketching possible layouts for your new kitchen, again using a scale of ½" equals 1 ft. As you develop your kitchen plan, refer often to your wish list of kitchen features and the kitchen standards and Code requirements listed early in this section. The goal is to create a kitchen that meets all your needs with the minimum possible impact on the present kitchen, because this will reduce the overall cost of your project.

3 If simple rearrangement of kitchen elements doesn't do the trick, explore the possibility of expanding your kitchen, either by enlarging the kitchen into an adjoining room, or by building a room addition. A kitchen designer or architect can help with this task.

4 Once you settle on a layout, use graph paper to draw a very detailed floor plan of your new kitchen. Use dotted lines to fill in the base cabinets and appliances, and solid lines to show the wall cabinets and countertops. (For straight runs of cabinets, leave a margin of about 3" to allow for adjustments during cabinet installation.) In the margins around the wall outline, indicate dimensions of kitchen elements and the distances between them.

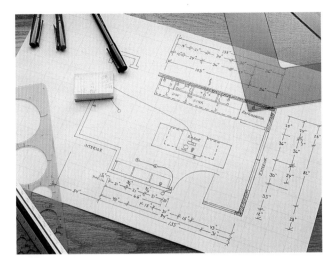

5 Use colored pencils to mark the locations of plumbing fixtures, electrical outlets, and lighting fixtures and the heating registers, radiators, or fixtures.

6 Draw a detailed, precise front elevation for each wall of your kitchen, using a scale of ½" equals 1 ft. Mark the vertical and horizontal measurements of all features, including doors, windows, wood moldings, cabinets, countertops, appliances, and soffits. Draw a side elevation of each wall of the kitchen, complete with all measurements. When satisfied with the elevation drawings, add the locations for plumbing pipes, electrical outlets, and lighting fixtures. Create close-up detail drawings of problem spots, such as the areas where appliances butt against window frames.

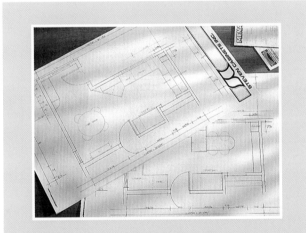

Tip

Although some homeowners have the artist's eye needed to draw accurate plans, others find this difficult if not impossible. If you fall into the latter category, don't be afraid to seek help. Home centers and cabinet manufacturers often have designers on staff who can help you draw up plans if you agree to buy materials from them. In addition, there are computer software programs that can help you develop accurate plans that can be printed out. And, of course, there are professional kitchen designers and architects who specialize in creating kitchen plans.

Wrapping Up

Once you've completed floor plans and elevation drawings of your kitchen-to-be, you're ready to begin choosing the appliances, cabinets, and other materials for your new kitchen. Create a detailed shopping list that includes dimensions and specifications for each item you'll be buying.

Now would be a good time to enlist the aid of an interior designer to help you select colors and patterns for flooring, countertops, and wall materials. Many installation contractors can also help you with design decisions.

Creating Plans

Use the icons shown below and the ¼" grid paper on the following pages to create working plans for your new kitchen. Use a scale of ½"= 1 ft. (1 square = 6") when drawing your plans; the icons are drawn to match this scale.

Plan view (overhead) templates for 24"-deep base cabinets

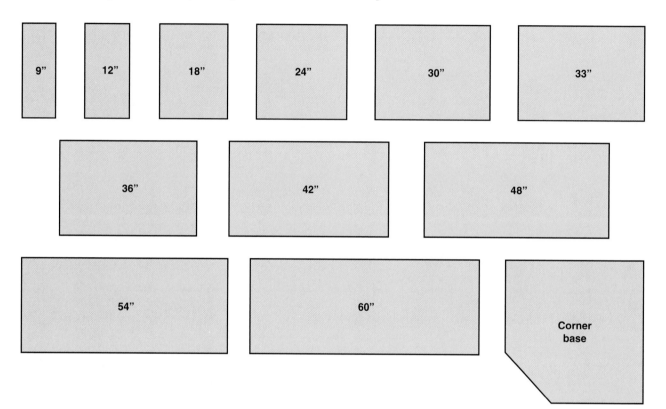

Plan view (overhead) templates for 12"-deep wall cabinets

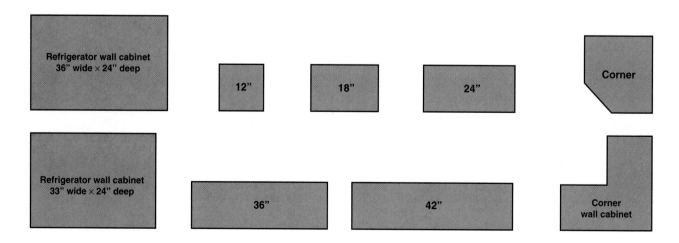

Basic construction symbols (not to scale)

Wall with insulation

Exterior door

Interior door

Folding door

Patio door

Double-hung window

Bay window

Skylight — SKY

Stairway

Electrical symbols

120-volt GFCI outlet — GFCI

Range outlet — R

Single-pole switch — S

Three-way switch — S₃

Vent fan — F

Thermostat — T

Telephone outlet

Incandescent ceiling fixture

Wall-mounted light fixture

Recessed light fixture — R

Fluorescent light fixture

Track light fixture

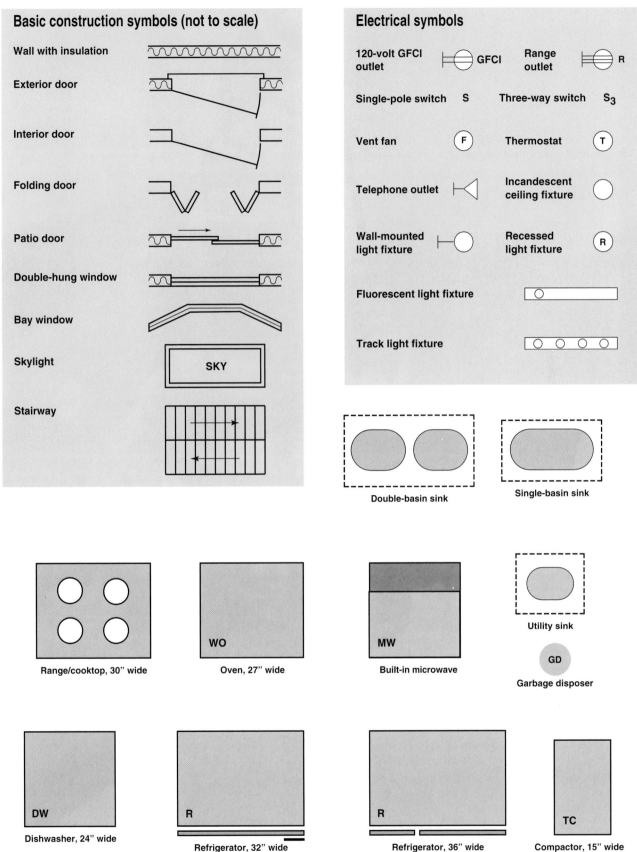

Double-basin sink

Single-basin sink

Range/cooktop, 30" wide

Oven, 27" wide — WO

Built-in microwave — MW

Utility sink

Garbage disposer — GD

Dishwasher, 24" wide — DW

Refrigerator, 32" wide — R

Refrigerator, 36" wide — R

Compactor, 15" wide — TC

Kitchen Remodeling
Techniques

Putty knives

Sanding block

Straightedge

Handscrew

Utility knife

Nail set

Dust mask

Standard screwdriver

Phillips screwdriver

Safety glasses

16-oz. claw hammer

Wonderbar®

Crosscut saw

Framing square

Combination square

C-clamps

Pencil

Tape measure

Bar clamp

Chalk line

Caulk gun

2' carpenter's level

Tools

A collection of quality tools does not require a large initial investment: a homeowner can build a tool collection by buying tools as they are needed for each project. Invest in top-grade tools made by reputable manufacturers. A quality tool always carries a full warranty.

Basic hand tools (photo, page opposite) are essential for the completion of most of the kitchen remodeling projects described in this book. A quality hand tool can last a lifetime, and over the years will be used many times for repairs and home improvement projects.

Basic power tools (photo, below) can increase the speed and precision of your kitchen improvement projects. Many power tools are made in cordless versions. Cordless tools can be used anywhere and are not restricted by electrical power connections.

When purchasing power tools, read specification labels to compare features. More horsepower, faster motor speeds, and higher amperage ratings indicate a well-engineered tool. Better-quality tools also have roller or ball bearings instead of sleeve bearings.

Circular saw

Belt sander

Finishing sander

Jig saw

Router

Cordless screwdriver

¾" power drill

Plumbing tools include: Propane torch with starter, solder paste, and lead-free solder (A), ratchet wrench with sockets (B), hacksaw (C), tubing cutter (D), ball peen hammer (E), wire brush (F), rubber mallet (G), file (H), channel-type pliers (I), adjustable wrenches (J), pipe wrenches (K).

Tools for Plumbing

The tools shown on this page are used in the plumbing work demonstrated in this book. You also will need some of the basic hand tools shown on page 30. We recommend that all do-it-yourself plumbers own these tools because you will use them extensively, both during the kitchen remodeling project and when making repairs in the future. If you purchase new tools, always invest in the highest quality tools you can afford.

You also may find certain power tools useful during plumbing work. A power miter box, jig saw, drill, and reciprocating saw can make the work easier and much quicker.

Occasionally, specialty tools will be required as part of a plumbing project. Tools such as an electric jackhammer for breaking concrete, a right-angle drill with a hole saw attachment, or a test kit for pressure-testing DWV pipes can be leased relatively inexpensively at a rental center.

Tools used in plumbing will very likely be exposed to water. Prevent rust by wiping your tools dry and applying a light coat of household oil after using them. Lubricants available in spray cans are convenient for this purpose.

Electrical tools include: Neon circuit tester (A), cable ripper (B), combination tool (C), needlenose pliers (D), linesman's pliers (E), screwdrivers with insulated handles (F), fish tape (G), utility knife (H), fuse puller (I), continuity tester (J).

Tools for Electrical Work

To complete the wiring projects shown in this book, you need a few specialty electrical tools (photo above), as well as the collection of basic hand tools shown on page 30. It will be most convenient if you own these tools so that you have them available for other electrical work and repairs—common occurrences in any home.

If you need to purchase these tools, they can be found in hardware stores and home improvement centers. As with any tool purchase, always buy the best tools you can afford. Keep your tools clean, and sharpen or replace any cutting tools that have dull edges.

You will find a tool belt dedicated to electrical tools is very helpful. It has multiple pockets and loops to hold the wide variety of tools and materials used in electrical work. Also, have several sizes of each type of screwdriver (slot and Phillips) in your tool belt. Screws common to electrical work come in many sizes.

You will need a few power tools when installing new wiring in a remodeled kitchen. Drills (having both corded and cordless on hand is very useful), a jig saw, and a reciprocating saw are necessary to run cable through framing members. You may find a right-angle drill is much easier to use when drilling holes. This can be found at a rental center.

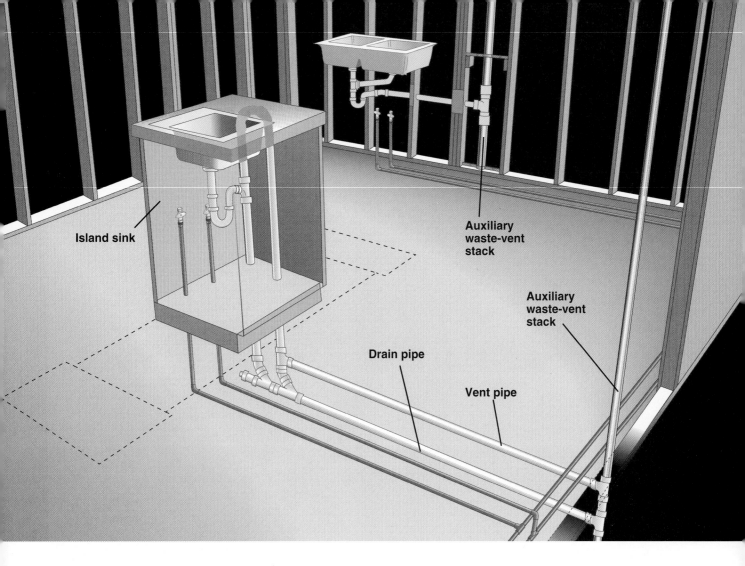

Island sink

Auxiliary waste-vent stack

Auxiliary waste-vent stack

Drain pipe

Vent pipe

Plumbing a Kitchen

Plumbing a remodeled kitchen is a relatively easy job if your kitchen includes only a wall sink. If your project includes an island sink, however, the work becomes more complicated.

An island sink poses problems because there is no adjacent wall in which to run a vent pipe. For an island sink, you will need to use a special plumbing configuration known as a *loop vent*.

Each loop vent situation is different, and your configuration will depend on the location of existing waste-vent stacks, the direction of the floor joists, and the size and location of your sink base cabinet. Consult your local plumbing inspector for help in laying out the loop vent.

Our demonstration kitchen includes a double wall sink and an island sink. The 1½" drain for the wall sink connects to an existing 2" galvanized waste-vent stack; since the trap is within 3½ ft. of the stack, no vent pipe is required. The drain for the island sink uses a loop vent configuration connected to an auxiliary waste-vent

Everything You Need

Tools: wire brush, drill with wire wheel attachment, cold chisel, hand maul, paint brush, trowel.

Materials: vinyl-reinforced patching compound, concrete caulk, sand-mix concrete.

stack in the basement.

The information on the following pages shows plumbing methods specific to a kitchen project. If you are not familiar with basic plumbing methods, find a good reference book to help you with this work.

For our demonstration kitchen, we have divided the project into three phases:
- How to Install DWV Pipes for a Wall Sink (pages 38 to 40)
- How to Install DWV Pipes for an Island Sink (pages 41 to 45)
- How to Install New Supply Pipes (pages 46 to 47)

Tips for Plumbing a Kitchen

Insulate exterior walls if you live in a region with freezing winter temperatures. Where possible, run water supply pipes through the floor or interior partition walls, rather than exterior walls.

Use existing waste-vent stacks to connect the new DWV pipes. In addition to a main waste-vent stack, most homes have one or more auxiliary waste-vent stacks in the kitchen that can be used to connect new DWV pipes.

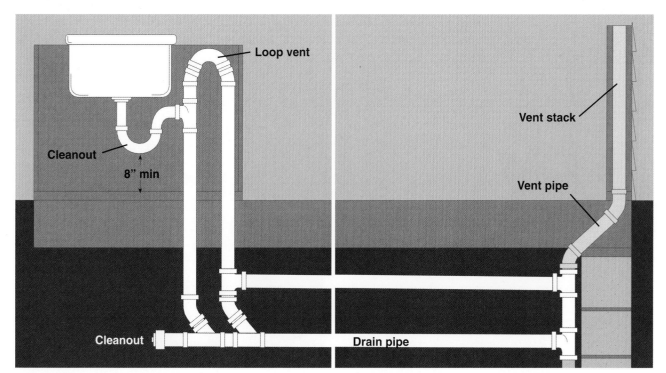

Loop vent makes it possible to vent a sink when there is no adjacent wall to house the vent pipe. The drain is vented with a loop of pipe that arches up against the countertop and away from the drain before dropping through the floor. The vent pipe then runs horizontally to an existing vent pipe. In our project, we have tied the island vent to a vent pipe extending up from a basement utility sink. NOTE: Loop vents are subject to local Code restrictions. Always consult your building inspector for guidelines on venting an island sink.

(continued next page)

Tips for Plumbing a Kitchen (continued)

A major plumbing project is a complicated affair requiring demolition and carpentry skills. Kitchen plumbing may be unusable for several days while completing the work, so make sure you have a backup kitchen space to use during this time. Always buy plenty of pipe and fittings—at least 25% more than you think you need. You can return the leftovers for credit. Making several extra trips to the building center for last-minute fittings is a nuisance, and it can add many hours of time to your project.

The how-to projects on the following pages demonstrate standard plumbing techniques, but should not be used as a literal blueprint for your work. Pipe and fitting sizes, fixture layout, and pipe routing will always vary according to individual circumstances. Before you begin work, create a detailed plumbing plan to guide your work and help you obtain the required permits.

Use 2 × 6 studs to frame "wet walls" when constructing a new kitchen. Thicker walls provide more room to run drain pipes and main waste-vent stacks, making installation much easier.

Consider the location of cabinets when roughing in the water supply and drain stub-outs. Read the layout specifications that come with each fixture or appliance, then mark the drain and supply lines accordingly.

Install control valves at the points where the new branch supply lines meet the main distribution pipes. By installing valves, you can continue to supply the rest of the house with water while you are working on the new branches.

Framing Member	Maximum Hole Size	Maximum Notch Size
2 × 4 loadbearing stud	1⁷⁄₁₆" diameter	⁷⁄₈" deep
2 × 4 non-loadbearing stud	2½" diameter	1⁷⁄₁₆" deep
2 × 6 loadbearing stud	2¼" diameter	1⅜" deep
2 × 6 non-loadbearing stud	3⁵⁄₁₆" diameter	2³⁄₁₆" deep
2 × 6 joists	1½" diameter	⁷⁄₈" deep
2 × 8 joists	2⅜" diameter	1¼" deep
2 × 10 joists	3¹⁄₁₆" diameter	1½" deep
2 × 12 joists	3¾" diameter	1⅞" deep

Framing member chart shows the maximum sizes for holes and notches that can be cut into studs and joists when running pipes. Where possible, use notches rather than bored holes, because pipe installation is usually easer. When boring holes, there must be at least ⅝" of wood between the edge of a stud and the hole, and at least 2" between the edge of a joist and the hole. Joists can be notched only in the end one-third of the overall span; never in the middle one-third of the joist. When two pipes are run through a stud, the pipes should be stacked one over the other, never side by side.

Create access panels so that in the future you will be able to service fixture fittings and shutoff valves located inside the walls. Frame an opening between studs, then trim the opening with wood moldings. Cover the opening with a removable plywood panel the same thickness as the wall surface, then finish it to match the surrounding walls.

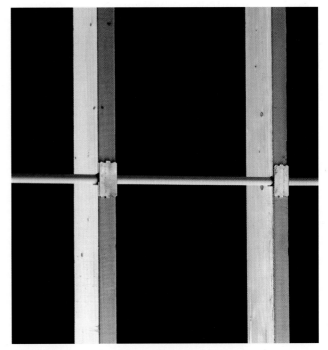

Protect pipes from punctures, if they are less than 1¼" from the front face of wall studs or joists, by attaching metal protector plates to the framing members.

How to Install DWV Pipes for a Wall Sink

1 Determine the location of the sink drain by marking the position of the sink and base cabinet on the floor. Mark a point on the floor indicating the position of the sink drain opening. This point will serve as a reference for aligning the sink drain stub-out.

2 Mark a route for the new drain pipe through the studs behind the wall sink cabinet. The drain pipe should angle ¼" per foot down toward the waste-vent stack.

3 Use a right-angle drill and hole saw to bore holes for the drain pipe (page 37). On non-loadbearing studs, such as the cripple studs beneath a window, you can notch the studs with a reciprocating saw to simplify the installation of the drain pipe. If the studs are loadbearing, however, you must thread the run though the bored holes, using couplings to join short lengths of pipe as you create the run.

4 Measure, cut, and dry-fit a horizontal drain pipe to run from the waste-vent stack to the sink drain stub-out. Create the stub-out with a 45° elbow and 6" length of 1½" pipe. NOTE: If the sink trap in your installation will be more than 3½ ft. from the waste-vent pipe, you will need to install a waste T and run a vent pipe up the wall, connecting it to the vent stack at a point at least 6" above the lip of the sink.

5 Remove the neoprene sleeve from a banded coupling, then roll the lip back and measure the thickness of the separator ring.

6 Attach two lengths of 2" pipe, at least 4" long, to the top and bottom openings on a 2" × 2" × 1½" waste T. Hold the fitting alongside the waste-vent stack, then mark the stack for cutting, allowing space for the separator rings on the banded couplings.

(continued next page)

7 Use riser clamps and 2 × 4 blocking to support the waste-vent stack above and below the new drain pipe, then cut out the waste-vent stack along the marked lines, using a reciprocating saw and metal-cutting blade.

8 Slide banded couplings onto the cut ends of the waste-vent stack, and roll back the lips of the neoprene sleeves. Position the waste T assembly, then roll the sleeves into place over the plastic pipes.

9 Slide the metal bands into place over the neoprene sleeves, and tighten the clamps with a ratchet wrench or screwdriver.

10 Solvent-glue the drain pipe, beginning at the waste-vent stack. Use a 90° elbow and a short length of pipe to create a drain stub-out extending about 4" out from the wall.

How to Install DWV Pipes for an Island Sink

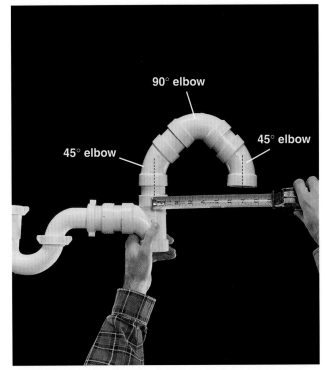

1 Position the base cabinet for the island sink, according to your kitchen plans. Mark the cabinet position on the floor with tape, then move the cabinet out of the way.

2 Create the beginning of the drain and loop vent by test-fitting a drain trap, waste T, two 45° elbows, and a 90° elbow, linking them with 2" lengths of pipe. Measure the width of the loop between the center-points of the fittings.

3 Draw a reference line perpendicular to the wall to use as a guide when positioning the drain pipes. A cardboard template of the sink can help you position the loop vent inside the outline of the cabinet.

4 Position the loop assembly on the floor, and use it as a guide for marking hole locations. Make sure to position the vent loop so the holes are not over joists.

(continued next page)

5 Use a hole saw with a diameter slightly larger than the vent pipes to bore holes in the subfloor at the marked locations. Note the positions of the holes by carefully measuring from the edges of the taped cabinet outline; these measurements will make it easier to position matching holes in the floor of the base cabinet.

6 Reposition the base cabinet, and mark the floor of the cabinet where the drain and vent pipes will run. (Make sure to allow for the thickness of the cabinet sides when measuring.) Use the hole saw to bore holes in the floor of the cabinet, directly above the holes in the subfloor.

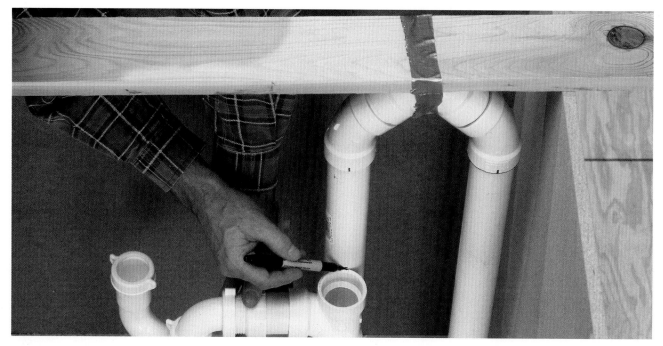

7 Measure, cut, and assemble the drain and loop vent assembly. Tape the top of the loop in place against a brace laid across the top of the cabinet, then extend the drain and vent pipes through the holes in the floor of the cabinet. The waste T should be about 18" above the floor, and the drain and vent pipes should extend about 2 ft. through the floor.

8 In the basement, establish a route from the island vent pipe to an existing vent pipe. (In our project, we are using the auxiliary waste-vent stack near a utility sink.) Hold a long length of pipe between the pipes, and mark for T-fittings. Cut off the plastic vent pipe at the mark, then dry-fit a waste T-fitting to the end of the pipe.

9 Hold a waste T against the vent stack, and mark the horizontal vent pipe at the correct length. Fit the horizontal pipe into the waste T, then tape the assembly in place against the vent stack. The vent pipe should angle ¼" per foot down toward the drain.

10 Fit a 3" length of pipe in the bottom opening on the T-fitting attached to the vent pipe, then mark both the vent pipe and the drain pipe for 45° elbows. Cut off the drain and vent pipes at the marks, then dry-fit the elbows onto the pipes.

11 Extend both the vent pipe and drain pipe by dry-fitting 3" lengths of pipe and Y-fittings to the elbows. Using a carpenter's level, make sure the horizontal drain pipe will slope toward the waste-vent at a pitch of ¼" per ft. Measure and cut a short length of pipe to fit between the Y-fittings.

(continued next page)

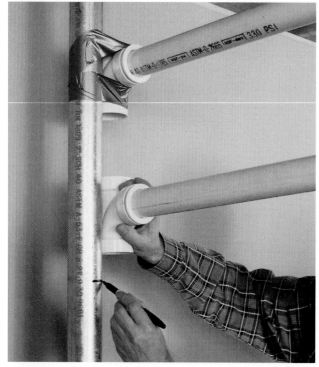

12 Cut a horizontal drain pipe to reach from the vent Y-fitting to the auxiliary waste-vent stack. Attach a waste T to the end of the drain pipe, then position it against the drain stack, maintaining a downward slope of ¼" per ft. Mark the auxiliary stack for cutting above and below the fittings.

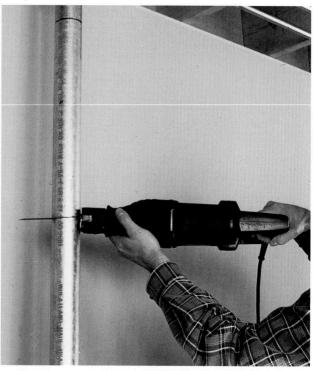

13 Cut out the auxiliary stack at the marks. Use the T-fittings and short lengths of pipe to assemble an insert piece to fit between the cutoff ends of the auxiliary stack. The insert assembly should be about ½" shorter than the removed section of stack.

14 Slide banded couplings onto the cut ends of the auxiliary stack, then insert the plastic pipe assembly and loosely tighten the clamps.

15 At the open inlet on the drain pipe Y-fitting, insert a cleanout fitting.

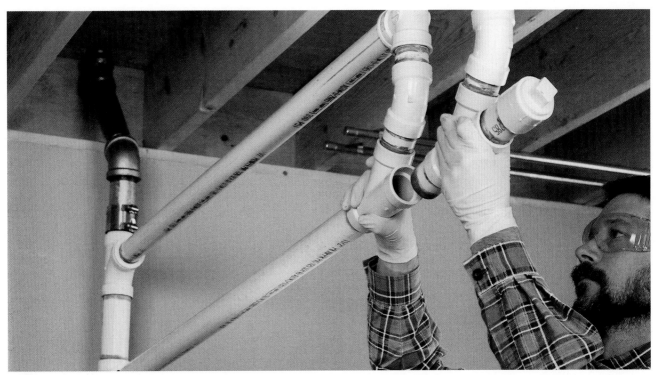

16 Solvent-glue all pipes and fittings found in the basement, beginning with the assembly inserted into the existing waste-vent stack, but do not glue the vertical drain and vent pipes running up into the cabinet. Tighten the banded couplings at the auxiliary stack. Support the horizontal pipes every 4 ft. with strapping nailed to the joists, then detach the vertical pipes extending up into the island cabinet. The final connection for the drain and vent loop will be completed as other phases of the kitchen remodeling project are finished.

17 After installing flooring and attaching cleats for the island base cabinet, cut away the flooring covering the holes for the drain and vent pipes.

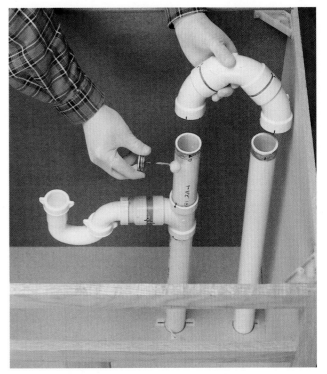

18 Install the base cabinet, then insert the drain and vent pipes through the holes in the cabinet floor and solvent-glue the pieces together.

How to Install New Supply Pipes

1 Drill two 1"-diameter holes, spaced about 6" apart, through the floor of the island base cabinet and the underlying subfloor. Position the holes so they are not over floor joists. Drill similar holes in the floor of the base cabinet for the wall sink.

2 Turn off the water at the main shutoff, and drain the pipes. Cut out any old water supply pipes that obstruct new pipe runs, using a tubing cutter or hacksaw. In our project, we are removing the old pipe back to a point where it is convenient to begin the new branch lines.

3 Dry-fit T-fittings on each supply pipe (we used ¾" × ½" × ½" reducing T-fittings). Use elbows and lengths of copper pipe to begin the new branch lines running to the island sink and the wall sink. The parallel pipes should be routed so they are between 3" and 6" apart.

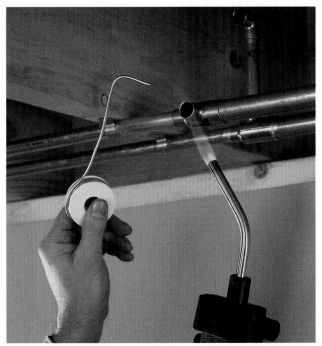

4 Solder the pipes and fittings together, beginning at the T-fittings. Support the horizontal pipe runs every 6 ft. with strapping attached to joists.

5 Extend the branch lines to points directly below the holes leading up into the base cabinets. Use elbows and lengths of pipe to form vertical risers extending at least 12" into the base cabinets. Use a small level to position the risers so they are plumb, then mark the pipe for cutting.

6 Fit the horizontal pipes and risers together, and solder them in place. Install blocking between joists, and anchor the risers to the blocking with pipe straps.

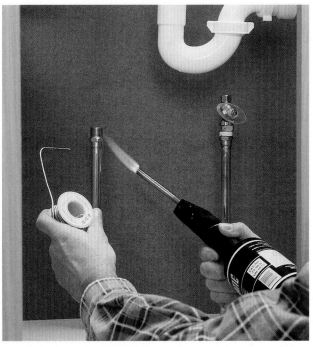

7 Solder male threaded adapters to the tops of the risers, then screw threaded shutoff valves onto the fittings.

14/2 cable

12/3 cable

6/3 cable

12/2 cable

14/2 cable

■ **#1 & #2: Small-appliance circuits.** Two 20-amp, 120-volt circuits supply power to countertop and eating areas for small appliances. All general-use receptacles must be on these circuits. One 12/3 cable, fed by a 20-amp double-pole breaker, wires both circuits. These circuits share one electrical box with the disposer circuit (#5), and another with the basic lighting circuit (#7).

■ **#3: Range circuit.** A 50-amp, 120/240-volt dedicated circuit supplies power to the range/oven appliance. It is wired with 6/3 cable.

■ **#4: Microwave circuit.** A dedicated 20-amp, 120 volt circuit supplies power to the microwave. It is wired with 12/2 cable. Microwaves that use less than 300 watts can be installed on a 15-amp circuit, or plugged into the small-appliance circuits.

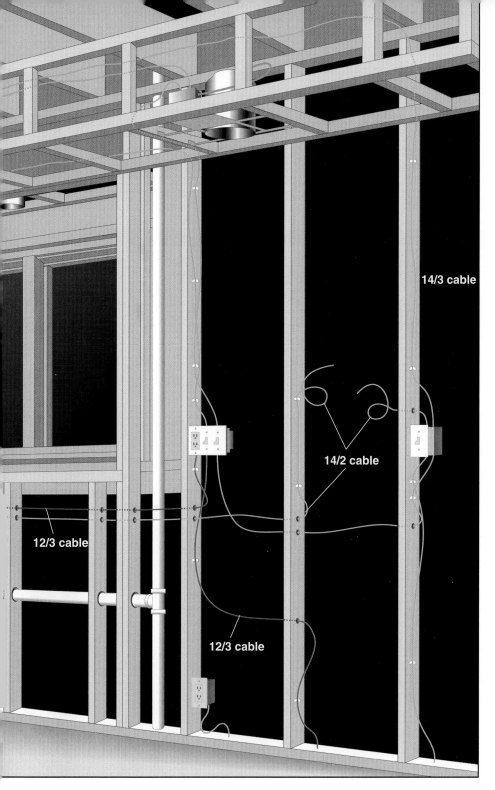

14/3 cable

14/2 cable

12/3 cable

12/3 cable

Wiring a Remodeled Kitchen

The kitchen remodeling wiring project shown on the following pages includes the installation of seven new circuits. Four of these are dedicated circuits: a 50-amp circuit supplying the range, a 20-amp circuit powering the microwave, and two 15-amp circuits supplying the diswasher and food disposer. In addition, two 20-amp circuits for small appliances supply power to all receptacles above the countertops and in the eating area. Finally, a 15-amp basic lighting circuit controls the ceiling fixture, all of the recessed fixtures, and the under-cabinet task lights.

All rough construction and plumbing work should be finished and inspected before beginning the electrical work. Divide the project into steps and complete each step before beginning the next.

The wiring information on the following pages concerns a kitchen project. If you are not familiar with basic wiring methods, see our Black & Decker® Home Improvement Library™ *Advanced Home Wiring*.

Three Steps for Wiring a Remodeled Kitchen:

- Plan the circuits (pages 50 to 51).
- Install boxes and cables (pages 52 to 55).
- Make final connections (pages 56 to 61).

Tools You Will Need:

Marker, tape measure, calculator, masking tape, screwdriver, hammer, power drill with 5/8" spade bit, cable ripper, combination tool, needlenose pliers, fish tape.

■ **#5: Food disposer circuit.** A dedicated 15-amp, 120-volt circuit supplies power to the disposer. It is wired with 14/2 cable. Some local Codes allow the disposer to be on the same circuit as the dishwasher.

■ **#6: Dishwasher circuit.** A dedicated 15-amp, 120-volt circuit supplies power to the dishwasher. It is wired with 14/2 cable. Some local Codes allow the dishwasher to be on the same circuit as the disposer.

■ **#7: Basic lighting circuit.** A dedicated 15-amp, 120-volt circuit powers the ceiling fixture, recessed fixtures, and under-cabinet task lights. 14/2 and 14/3 cables connect the fixtures and switches in the circuit. Each task light has a self-contained switch.

4 ft. maximum

Code requires receptacles above countertops to be no more than 4 ft. apart. Put receptacles closer together in areas where many appliances will be used. Any section of countertop that is wider than 12" must have a receptacle located above it. (Countertop spaces separated by items such as range tops, sinks, and refrigerators are considered separate sections.) All accessible receptacles in kitchens (and bathrooms) must be a GFCI. On walls without countertops, receptacles should be no more than 12 ft. apart.

Plan the Circuits

A kitchen generally uses more power than other rooms because it contains many light fixtures and appliances. Where you locate these items depends upon your needs. Make sure the main work areas of your kitchen have plenty of light and enough receptacles. Try to anticipate future needs: for example, install a range receptacle when remodeling, even if you currently have a gas range. It is difficult and expensive to make changes later.

Contact your local Building and Electrical Code offices before you begin planning. They may have requirements that differ from the National Electrical Code. Remember that the Code contains minimum requirements primarily concerning safety, not convenience or need. Work with the inspectors to create a safe plan that also meets your needs.

To help locate receptacles, plan carefully where cabinets and appliances will be in the finished project. Appliances installed within cabinets, such as microwaves or food disposers, must have their receptacles positioned according to manufacturer's instructions. Put at least one receptacle at table height in the dining areas for convenience in operating a small appliance.

The ceiling fixture should be centered in the kitchen ceiling. Or, if your kitchen contains a dining area or breakfast nook, you may want to center the light fixture over the table. Locate recessed light fixtures and under-cabinet task lights where they will best illuminate main work areas.

Before drawing diagrams and applying for a permit, evaluate your existing service and make sure it provides enough power to supply the new circuits you are planning to add. If you find that it will not, contact a licensed electrician to upgrade your service before beginning your work.

Bring the wiring plan and materials list to the inspector's office when applying for the permit. If the inspector suggests improvements to your plan, such as using switches with grounding screws, follow his advice. He can save you time and money.

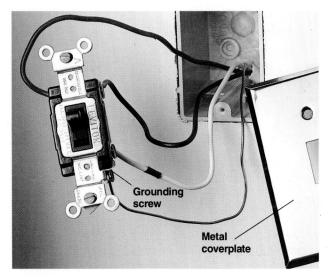

Grounding screw

Metal coverplate

A switch with a grounding screw may be required by inspectors in kitchens and baths. Code requires them when metal coverplates are used with plastic boxes.

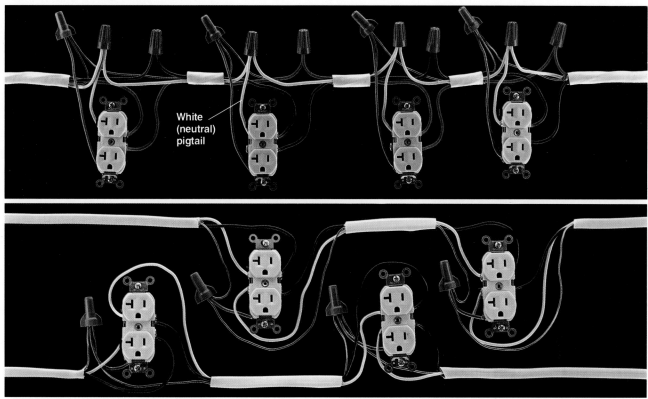

White (neutral) pigtail

Two 20-amp small-appliance circuits can be wired with one 12/3 cable supplying power to both circuits (top), rather than using separate 12/2 cables for each circuit (bottom), to save time and money. Because these circuits must be GFCI protected, either place a GFCI receptacle first in each circuit (the remaining 20-amp duplex units are connected through the LOAD terminals on the GFCI) or use a GFCI receptacle at each location. In 12/3 cable, the black wire supplies power to one circuit for alternate receptacles (the first, third, etc.), the red wire supplies power for the second circuit to the remaining receptacles. The white wire is the neutral for both circuits. For safety, it must be attached with a pigtail to each receptacle, instead of being connected directly to the terminal. These circuits must contain all general-use receptacles in the kitchen, pantry, breakfast area, or dining room. No lighting outlets or receptacles from any other rooms can be connected to them.

Work areas at sink and range should be well lighted for convenience and safety. Install switch-controlled lights over these areas.

Ranges require a dedicated 40- or 50-amp 120/240-volt circuit (or two circuits for separate oven and counter-top units). Even if you do not have an electric range, it is a good idea to install the circuit when remodeling.

Dishwashers and food disposers require dedicated 15-amp, 120-volt circuits in most local Codes. Some inspectors will allow these appliances to share one circuit.

Heights of electrical boxes in a kitchen vary depending upon their use. In the kitchen project shown here the centers of the boxes above the countertop are 45" above the floor, in the center of 18" backsplashes that extend from the countertop to the cabinets. All boxes for wall switches also are installed at this height.

The center of the box for the microwave receptacle is 72" off the floor, where it will fit between the cabinets. The centers of the boxes for the range and food disposer receptacles are 12" off the floor, but the center of the box for the dishwasher receptacle is 6" off the floor, next to the space the appliance will occupy.

Install Boxes & Cables

After the inspector issues you a work permit, you can begin installing electrical boxes for switches, receptacles, and fixtures. Install all boxes and frames for recessed fixtures such as vent fans and recessed lights before cutting and installing any cable. However, some surface-mounted fixtures, such a s under-cabinet task lights, have self-contained wire connection boxes. These fixtures are installed after the walls are finished and the cabinets are in place.

First determine locations for the boxes above the countertops (page opposite). After establishing the height for these boxes, install all of the other visible wall boxes at this height. Boxes that will be behind appliances or inside cabinets should be located according to appliance manufacturer's

instructions. For example, the receptacle for the dishwasher cannot be installed directly behind the appliance; it is often located in the sink cabinet for easy access.

Always use the largest electrical boxes that are practical for you installation. Using large boxes ensures that you will meet Code regulations concerning box volume, and simplifies making the connections.

After all the boxes and recessed fixtures are installed, you are ready to measure and cut the cables. First install the feeder cables that run from the circuit breaker panel to the first electrical box in each circuit. Then cut and install the remaining cables to complete the circuits.

Tips for Installing Boxes & Cables

Install switch boxes at accessible locations, with the center of the box 48" from the floor. Position each box so the front face will be flush with the finished wall, and drive the mounting nails into the stud.

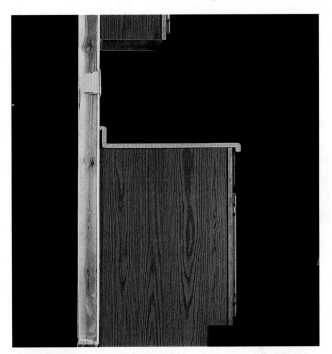

Standard backsplash height is 4"; the center of a box installed above this should be 44" above the floor. If the backsplash is more than 4" height, or the distance between the countertop and the bottom of the cabinet is less than 18", center the box in the space between the countertop and the bottom of the wall cabinet.

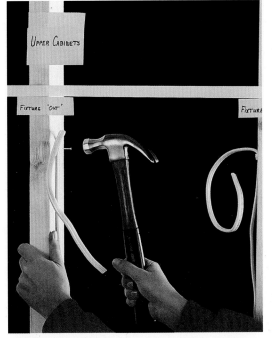

Install cables for an under-cabinet light at positions that will line up with the knockouts on the fixture box (which is installed after the walls and cabinets are in place). Cables will be retrieved through 5/8" drilled holes (page 61), so it is important to position the cables accurately.

Choose the proper type of recessed light fixture for your project. There are two types of fixtures: those rated for installation within insulation (left), and those which must be kept at least 3" from insulation (right). Self-contained thermal switches shut off power if the unit gets too hot for its rating. A recessed light fixture must be installed at least 1/2" from combustible materials.

How to Mount a Recessed Light Fixture

1 Extend the mounting bars on the recessed fixture to reach the framing members. Adjust the position of the light unit on the mounting bars to locate it properly. Align the bottom edges of the mounting bars with the bottom face of the framing members.

2 Nail or screw the mounting bars to the framing members.

3 Remove the wire connection box cover and open one knockout for each cable entering the box.

4 Install a cable clamp for each open knockout, and tighten locknut, using a screwdriver to drive the lugs.

How to Install the Feeder Cable

Sill plate

Cutaway view

1 Drill access holes through the sill plate where the feeder cables will enter from the circuit breaker panel. Choose spots that offer easy access to the circuit breaker panel as well as to the first electrical box on the circuit.

2 Drill 5/8" holes through framing members to allow cables to pass from the circuit breaker panel to access holes. Front edge of hole should be at least 1 1/4" from front edge of framing member.

3 For each circuit, measure and cut enough cable to run from circuit breaker panel, through access hole into the kitchen, to the first electrical box in the circuit. Add at least 2 ft. for the panel and 1 ft. for the box.

Cutaway view

4 Anchor the cable with a cable staple within 12" of the panel. Extend cable through and along joists to access hole into kitchen, stapling every 4 ft. where necessary. Keep cable at least 1 1/4" from front edge of framing members. Thread cable through access hole into kitchen, and on to the first box in the circuit. Continue circuit to rest of boxes.

Arrange for the rough-in inspection before making the final connections.

Make Final Connections

Make the final connections for switches, receptacles, and fixtures after the rough-in inspection. First, make final connections on recessed fixtures (it is easier to do this before wallboard is installed). Then, finish the work on walls and ceiling, install the cabinets, and make the rest of the final connections. Use the photos on the following pages as a guide for making the final connections. The last step is to connect the circuits at the breaker panel. After all connections are made, your work is ready for the final inspection.

Materials You Will Need:

Pigtail wires, wire nuts, black tape.

■ Circuits #1 & #2
Two 20-amp, 120-volt small-appliance circuits.

- 7 GFCI receptacles
- 20-amp double-pole circuit breaker

Note: In this project, two of the GFCI receptacles are installed in boxes that also contain switches from other circuits (page opposite).

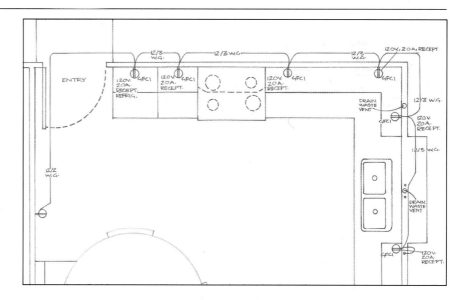

How to Connect Small-appliance Receptacles (that alternate on two 20-amp circuits in one 12/3 cable)

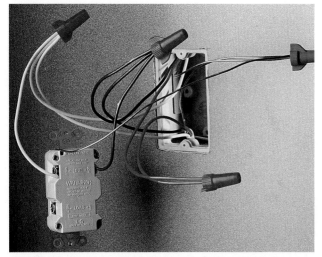

1 At alternate receptacles in the cable run (first, third, etc.), attach a black pigtail to brass screw terminal marked LINE on the receptacle and to black wire from both cables. Connect a white pigtail to a silver screw (LINE) and to both white wires. Connect a grounding pigtail to the grounding screw and to both grounding wires. Connect both red wires together. Tuck wires into box, then attach the receptacle and coverplate.

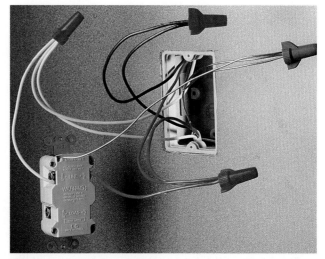

2 At remaining receptacles in the run, attach a red pigtail to a brass screw terminal (LINE) and to red wires from the cables. Attach a white pigtail to a silver screw terminal (LINE) and to both white wires. Connect a grounding pigtail to the grounding screw and to both grounding wires. Connect both black wires together. Tuck wires into box, attach receptacle and coverplate. (See page 51 for optional method of GFCI protection.)

How to Install a GFCI & a Disposer Switch

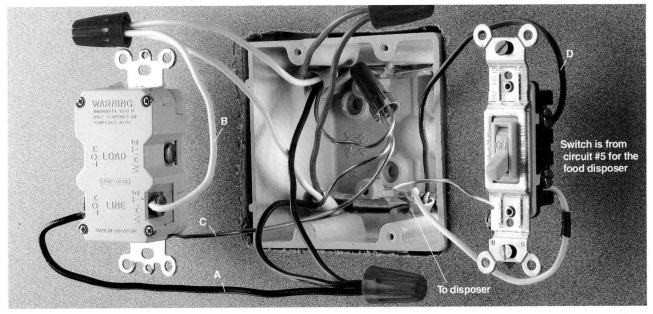

Connect black pigtail (A) to GFCI brass terminal marked LINE, and to black wires from three-wire cables. Attach white pigtail (B) to silver terminal marked LINE, and to white wires from three-wire cables. Attach grounding pigtail (C) to GFCI grounding screw and to grounding wires from three-wire cables. Connect both red wires together. Connect black wire from two-wire cable (D) to one switch terminal. Attach white wire to other terminal and tag it black indicating it is hot. Attach grounding wire to switch grounding screw. Tuck wires into box, attach switch, receptacle, and coverplate.

How to Install a GFCI & Two Switches for Recessed Lights

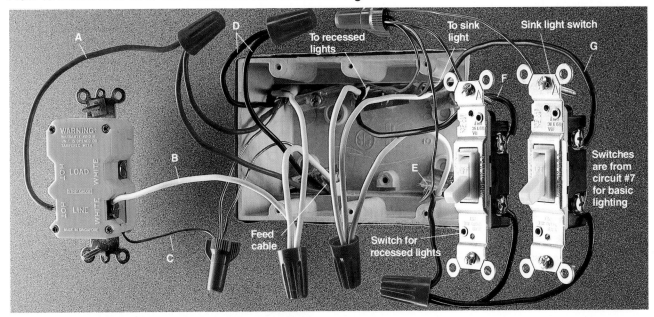

Connect red pigtail (A) to GFCI brass terminal labeled LINE, and to red wires from three-wire cables. Connect white pigtail (B) to silver LINE terminal, and to white wires from three-wire cables. Attach grounding pigtail (C) to grounding screw, and to grounding wires from three-wire cables. Connect black wires from three-wire cables (D) together. Attach a black pigtail to one screw on each switch and to black wire from two-wire feed cable (E).

Connect black wire (F) from the two-wire cable leading to recessed lights to remaining screw on the switch for the recessed lights. Connect black wire (G) from two-wire cable leading to sink light to remaining screw on sink light switch. Connect white wires from all two-wire cables together. Connect pigtails to switch grounding screws, and to all grounding wires from two-wire cables. Tuck wires into box, attach switches, receptacle, and coverplate.

Circuit #3

A 50-amp, 120/240-volt circuit serving the range.

- 50-amp receptacle for range
- 50-amp double-pole circuit breaker

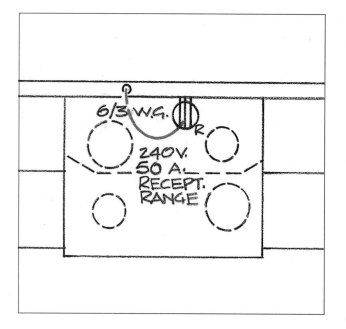

How to Install 120/240 Range Receptacle

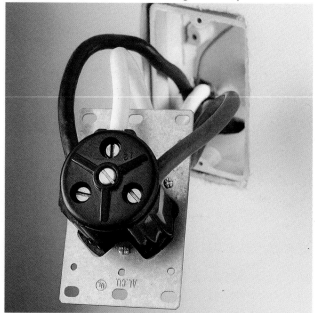

Attach the white wire to the neutral terminal, and the black and red wires to the remaining terminals. The neutral white wire acts as the grounding wire for this circuit, so push the bare copper ground wire from the cable to the back of the box. Tuck rest of the wires into the box. Attach receptacle and coverplate.

Circuit #4

A 20-amp, 120-volt circuit for the microwave.

- 20-amp duplex receptacle
- 20-amp single-pole circuit breaker

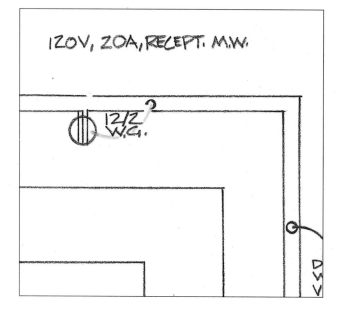

How to Connect Microwave Receptacle

Connect black wire from the cable to a brass screw terminal on the receptacle. Attach the white wire to a silver screw terminal, and the grounding wire to the receptacle's grounding screw. Tuck wires into box, attach the receptacle and the coverplate.

■ Circuit #5
A 15-amp, 120-volt circuit for the food disposer.

- 15-amp duplex receptacle
- Single-pole switch
- 15 amp single-pole circuit breaker

Note: Final connection of the single-pole switch controlling the disposer is shown on page 57.

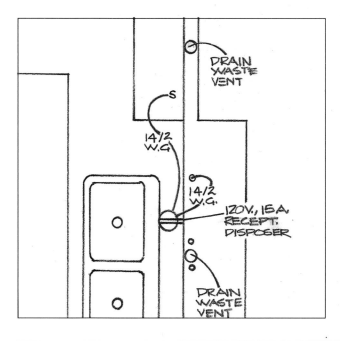

How to Connect Disposer Receptacle

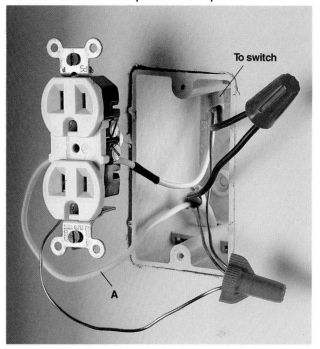

Connect black wires together. Connect white wire from feed cable (A) to silver screw on receptacle. Connect white wire from cable going to the switch to a brass screw terminal on the receptacle, and tag the wire with black indicating it is hot. Attach a grounding pigtail to grounding screw and to both cable grounding wires. Tuck wires into box, then attach receptacle and coverplate.

■ Circuit #6
A 15-amp, 120-volt circuit for the dishwasher.

- 15-amp duplex receptacle
- 15 amp single-pole circuit breaker

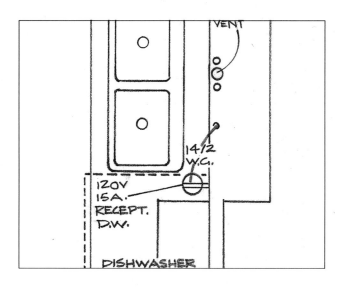

How to Connect Dishwasher Receptacle

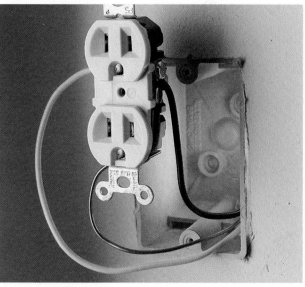

Connect the black wire to a brass screw terminal. Attach the white wire to a silver screw terminal. Connect the grounding wire to the grounding screw. Tuck wires into box, then attach receptacle and coverplate.

Circuit #7

A 15-amp basic lighting circuit serving the kitchen.

- 2 three-way switches with grounding screws
- 2 single-pole switches with grounding screws
- Ceiling light fixture
- 6 recessed light fixtures
- 4 flourescent under-cabinet fixtures
- 15 amp single-pole circuit breaker

Note: Final connections for the single-pole switches are shown on page 57.

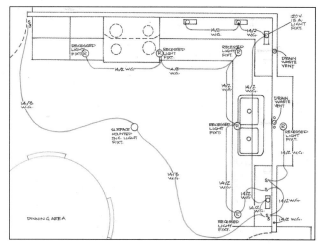

How to Connect First Three-way Switch

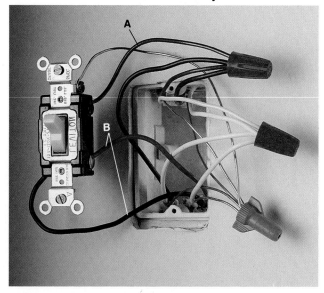

Connect a black pigtail to the common screw on the switch (A) and to the black wires from the two-wire cable. Connect black and red wires from the three-wire cable to traveler terminals (B) on the switch. Connect white wires from all cables entering box together. Attach a grounding pigtail to switch grounding screw and to all grounding wires in box. Tuck wires into box, then attach switch and coverplate.

How to Connect Surface-mounted Ceiling Fixture

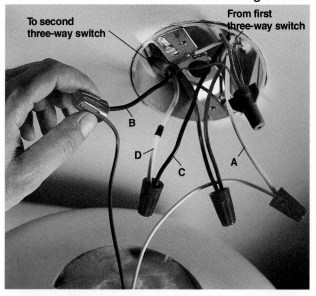

Connect white fixture lead to white wire (A) from first three-way switch. Connect black fixture lead to black wire (B) from second three-way switch. Connect black wire (C) from first switch to white wire (D) from second switch, and tag this white wire with black. Connect red wires from both switches together. Connect all grounding wires together. Mount fixture following manufacturer's instructions.

How to Connect Second Three-way Switch

Connect black wire from the cable to the common screw terminal (A). Connect red wire to one traveler screw terminal. Attach the white wire to the other traveler screw terminal and tag it with black, indicating it is hot. Attach the grounding wire to the grounding screw on the switch. Tuck wires in box, then attach switch and coverplate.

How to Connect Recessed Light Fixtures

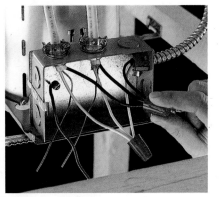

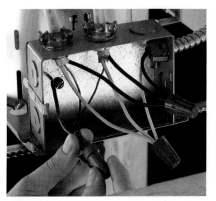

1 Make connections before installing wallboard: the work must be inspected first and access to the junction box is easier. Connect white cable wires to white fixture lead.

2 Connect black wires to black lead from fixture.

3 Attach a grounding pigtail to the grounding screw on the fixture, then connect all grounding wires. Tuck wires into the junction box, and replace the cover.

How to Connect Under-cabinet Fluorescent Task Light Fixtures

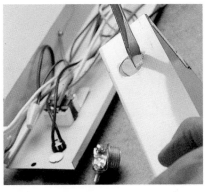

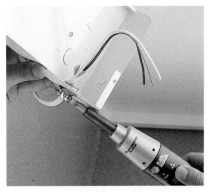

1 Drill 5/8" holes through wall and cabinet at locations that line up with knockouts on the fixture, and retrieve cable ends (page 53).

2 Remove access cover on fixture. Open one knockout for each cable that enters fixture box, and install cable clamps.

3 Strip 8" of sheathing from each cable end. Insert each end through a cable clamp, leaving 1/4" of sheathing in fixture box.

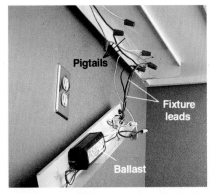

4 Screw fixture box to cabinet. Attach black, white, and green pigtails of THHN/THWN wire to wires from one cable entering box. Pigtails must be long enough to reach the cable at other end of box.

5 Connect black pigtail and circuit wire to black lead from fixture. Connect white pigtail and circuit wire to white lead from fixture. Attach green pigtail and copper circuit wire to green grounding wire attached to the fixture box.

6 Tuck wires into box, and route THHN/THWN pigtails along one side of the ballast. Replace access cover and fixture lens.

Make hookups at circuit breaker panel and arrange for the final inspection.

Flooring

Give your kitchen a fresh look with new flooring. There are many floor covering products available that are rugged, beautiful, and designed especially for do-it-yourself installations.

Resilient vinyl floor coverings are good choices for kitchens. They resist moisture, and many of them are manufactured with a cushioned backing for added comfort. Resilient tile is one of the easiest floor surfaces to install. Resilient sheet goods can often be installed in a single piece, eliminating seams and preventing moisture from seeping through to the subfloor.

Hardwood flooring is available as strips, planks, or parquet tiles that come prefinished with coats of tough polyurethane. Prefinished wood flooring locks together with a tongue-and-groove edges, and is installed over a troweled-on adhesive or thing sheets of foam rubber.

Plastic laminated flooring looks like a wood floor and is installed with methods similar to those for veneered wood planks. It is extremely durable and comes in a wide range of styles.

Ceramic tile offers a wide variety of patterns, styles, and colors that can complement any room. Properly installed ceramic tile has timeless elegance and is one of the most durable floor coverings available.

Planning for a New Floor Covering

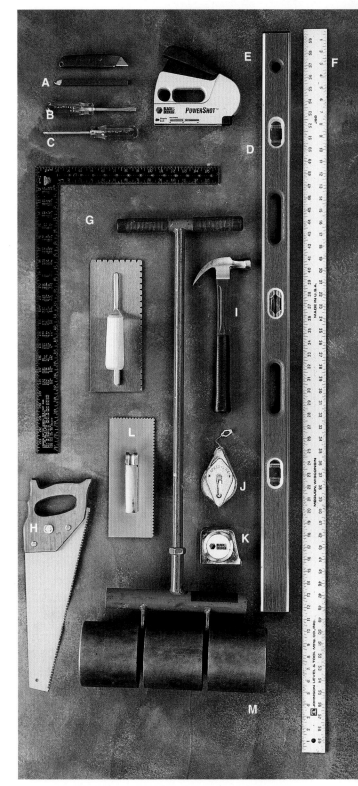

New floor coverings can be installed directly over existing surfaces that are flat, level, and well bonded. Damaged, worn, or loose flooring can be removed, or repaired and covered with plywood underlayment to provide a suitable base for new floor coverings.

In some instances, the addition of new flooring and plywood underlayment may interfere with the replacement of appliances. In these cases, the old flooring must be removed.

Carefully examine your old floor to determine what preparation, if any, must be completed before you install new flooring. Refer to the guidelines (right). Then measure your kitchen floor accurately to determine the quantity of new materials required.

Guidelines for Preparing Your Existing Floor

Resilient tile or sheet goods: New flooring can be installed directly over resilient goods. Cushioned or embossed resilient goods must be removed or covered with plywood.

Strip, plank, or parquet wood flooring: Roughen surface with sandpaper to remove gloss. Fill cracks with plastic filler and sand smooth. Damaged or warped wood floors should be sanded level and covered with plywood underlayment.

Ceramic tile: Roughen surface with 120-grit sandpaper to remove gloss. Level entire surface with latex underlayment, allow underlayment to dry, and sand smooth. New resilient sheet goods cannot be stapled to ceramic tile (page 74). Use flooring adhesive instead of staples.

Carpet: Always remove carpeting before installing new floor coverings.

Wood subfloors: Must be at least ¾" thick. Install ceramic tile over plywood subfloors that are at least 1⅛" total thickness.

Concrete slab subfloors: Consult a professional contractor to determine the condition of the slab.

Basic hand tools needed for most floor projects include: utility knife (A), pencil (B), standard and phillips screwdrivers (C), stapler (D), carpenter's level (E), straightedge (F), carpenter's square (G), hand saw (H), hammer (I), chalkline (J), and tape measure (K).

Specialty tools for flooring installation include: notched trowels (L), linoleum roller (M), and others as indicated.

63

Selecting Underlayment Materials

Which type of underlayment you should choose depends in part on the type of floor covering you will be installing. For example, ceramic and natural-stone floors require a rigid and stable underlayment that resists movement, such as cementboard. For resilient flooring, use a quality-grade plywood, since most manufacturers will void their warranty if their flooring is installed over substandard underlayment. Solid wood strip flooring and carpet do not require underlayment and are often placed directly on a plywood subfloor.

Plywood (A) is the most common underlayment for resilient flooring and ceramic tile installations. For resilient flooring, use ¼" exterior-grade, AC plywood (at least one side perfectly smooth). Wood-based floor coverings, like parquet, can be installed over lower-quality exterior-grade plywood. For ceramic tile, use ½" AC plywood. Most manufacturers now recommend plywood over other wood-based, sheet-good underlayments.

Fiber/cementboard (B) is a thin, high-density underlayment used under ceramic tile and resilient flooring in situations where floor height is a concern. (For installation, follow steps for cementboard installation, page 66.)

Cementboard (C) is used only for ceramic tile installations. It is completely stable, even when wet, and is therefore the best underlayment to use in areas likely to get wet, such as bathrooms. Cementboard is considerably more expensive than plywood.

Isolation membrane (D) is used to protect ceramic tile installations from movement that may occur on cracked concrete floors. It is used primarily for covering individual cracks with strips of membrane, but it can also be used over an entire floor. A specialty product, it is available from commercial tile distributors.

Latex patching compounds can be used to fill cracks and chips in old underlayment as well as to cover screw or nail heads and seams in new underlayment. Some products include separate dry and wet ingredients that need to be mixed before application; others are premixed.

How to Install Plywood Underlayment

1 Begin installing full sheets of plywood along the longest wall, making sure underlayment seams are not aligned with subfloor seams. Fasten plywood to the subfloor, using 1" screws driven every 6" along the edges and at 8" intervals throughout the rest of the sheet.

2 Continue fastening plywood to the subfloor, driving screw heads slightly below the underlayment surface. Leave ¼" expansion gaps at the walls and between sheets. Offset seams in subsequent rows.

3 Using a circular saw or jig saw, notch underlayment sheets to meet existing flooring in doorways, then fasten notched sheets to the subfloor.

4 Mix floor patching compound and latex or acrylic additive, according to manufacturer's directions. Then, spread it over seams and screw heads with a wallboard knife.

5 Let patching compound dry, then sand patched areas smooth, using a power sander.

How to Install Cementboard or Fiber/Cementboard Underlayment

1 Mix thin-set mortar according to manufacturer's recommendations. Starting at the longest wall, spread mortar on subfloor in a figure-eight pattern with a ¼" notched trowel. Spread only enough mortar for one sheet at a time. Set the cementboard sheet on the mortar, smooth-face up, making sure the edges are offset from subfloor seams.

2 Fasten cementboard to subfloor, using 1½" deck screws driven every 6" along edges and 8" throughout sheet; drive screw heads flush with surface. Continue spreading mortar and installing sheets along the wall. OPTION: If installing fiber/cement underlayment, use a ³⁄₁₆" notched trowel to spread mortar, and drill pilot holes for all screws.

3 Cut cementboard pieces to fit, leaving a slight gap at the joints. For straight cuts, score a line with a utility knife, then snap the board along the score.

4 To cut holes, notches, or irregular shapes, use a jig saw with a carbide blade. Continue installing cementboard sheets to cover the entire floor.

5 Place fiberglass mesh tape over seams, and spread a thin layer of thin-set mortar over the tape with a wallboard knife, feathering the edges. Allow mortar to cure for two days before proceeding with tile installation.

How to Install Isolation Membrane

1 Thoroughly clean the subfloor, then apply thin-set mortar with a ⅛" notched trowel. Start spreading the mortar along a wall in a section as wide as the membrane, and 8 to 10 ft. long. NOTE: For some membranes, you must use a bonding material other than mortar. Read the directions on the label.

2 Roll out the membrane over the mortar. Cut the membrane to fit tightly against the walls, using a straightedge and utility knife.

3 Starting in the center of the membrane, use a linoleum roller to smooth out the surface toward the edges. This frees trapped air and presses out excess bonding material.

4 Repeat steps 1 through 3, cutting membrane as necessary at the walls, until the floor is completely covered with membrane. Do not overlap seams, but make sure they are tight. Allow mortar to cure for two days before installing tile.

Solid vinyl

Vinyl composition flooring

Printed vinyl flooring

Most resilient flooring is made at least in part from vinyl. In general, the higher the percentage of vinyl in the product, the higher the quality of the tile. In solid vinyl flooring, the design pattern is built up from solid layers of vinyl. Vinyl composition flooring combines vinyl with filler materials. Printed vinyl flooring relies on a screen print for its color and pattern; the print is protected by a vinyl and urethane wear layer.

Resilient Flooring

Resilient flooring is often designed to mimic the look of ceramic tile or terrazzo, but is much easier to install and far less expensive. It is available both in sheets and tiles. Sheet vinyl comes in 6- and 12-foot-wide rolls. Most vinyl tiles are 1-foot squares, though some manufacturers make 9-inch square tiles and thin, 2-foot-long border strips.

Sheet vinyl is a good choice for kitchens since it has few seams for water to seep through; in smaller rooms, you can install sheet vinyl with no seams at all. Vinyl tiles perform best in dry locations, where a floor with many seams is not a liability.

The quality of resilient flooring varies significantly, and is based primarily on the amount of vinyl in the material. Solid vinyl is the best and most expensive flooring. In this type, the pattern is created by embedding colored vinyl pieces in a vinyl base. Vinyl composition products are less expensive than solid vinyl products. In composition flooring, the pattern is created by fusing colored vinyl with nonvinyl fillers. With both solid vinyl and vinyl composition flooring, the thickness of the flooring is a good clue to its quality; thicker materials have more vinyl and are therefore more durable.

Unlike traditional solid and composition vinyl materials, printed flooring gets its color and pattern from the print itself, which has no vinyl content. Instead, printed flooring is manufactured with a wear layer of urethane and vinyl. The thicker the wear layer, the better the quality of the flooring.

Resilient sheet vinyl comes in full-spread and perimeter-bond styles. Full-spread sheet vinyl has a felt-paper backing, and is secured with adhesive that is spread over the floor before installation. Perimeter-bond flooring, identifiable by its smooth, white PVC backing, is laid directly on underlayment and is secured by a special adhesive spread along the edges and seams.

Full-spread vinyl flooring bonds tightly to the floor and is unlikely to come loose, but it is more difficult to install and requires a flawlessly smooth and clean underlayment.

Perimeter-bond flooring, by contrast, is easier to install and will tolerate some minor underlayment flaws. However, it is also more likely to come loose.

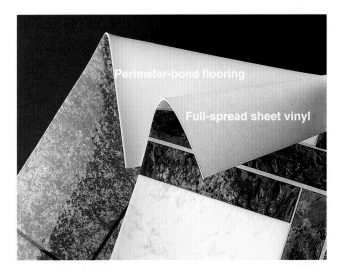

Resilient tile comes in self-adhesive and dry-back styles. Self-adhesive tile has a preapplied adhesive protected by a wax-paper backing that is peeled off as the tiles are installed. Dry-back tile is secured with adhesive spread onto the underlayment before installation.

Self-adhesive tile is easier to install than dry-back tile, but the bond is less reliable. Do not use additional adhesives with self-adhesive tile.

Tips for Working with Resilient Flooring

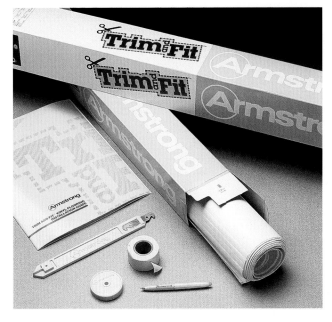

Make a template of the room perimeter to ensure an exact fit for a sheet vinyl installation. Some flooring manufacturers offer template kits and may even guarantee the installation if you use their kit.

Use a linoleum knife or a utility knife to cut resilient flooring. Make sure the knife blade is sharp, and change blades often. Always make cuts on a smooth surface, such as a scrap of hardboard.

Installing Resilient Sheet Vinyl

The most important phase of a sheet vinyl installation is creating a near-perfect underlayment surface. Another key to a successful installation is cutting the material so it fits perfectly along the contours of a room. Making a cutting template is the best way to ensure that your cuts will be correct (opposite page). When handling sheet vinyl, remember that this product—especially felt-backed—can crease and tear easily if mishandled.

Make sure you use the recommended adhesive for the sheet vinyl you are installing. Many manufacturers require that you use their glue to install their flooring, and will void their warranties if you do not follow their directions exactly. Apply adhesive sparingly, using a ⅛" or ¼" trowel.

Everything You Need:

Tools: basic hand tools, linoleum knife, compass, scissors, wallboard knife, J-roller, 100-lb. floor roller (for full-spread).

Materials: template paper, masking tape, duct tape, flooring adhesive, metal threshold.

How to Make a Cutting Template

1 Place sheets of heavy butcher's or postal-wrap paper along the walls, leaving a ⅛" gap. Cut triangular holes in the paper with a utility knife. Fasten the template to the floor by placing masking tape over the holes.

2 Follow the outline of the room, working with one sheet of paper at a time. Overlap the edges of adjoining sheets by about 2", and tape the sheets together.

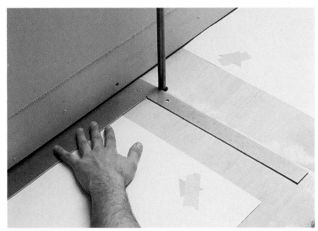

3 To fit the template around pipes, tape sheets of paper on either side. Measure the distance from the wall to the center of the pipe, and subtract ⅛".

4 Transfer the measurement to a separate piece of paper. Use a compass to draw the pipe diameter onto the paper, then cut out the hole with scissors or a utility knife. Cut a slit from the edge of the paper to the hole.

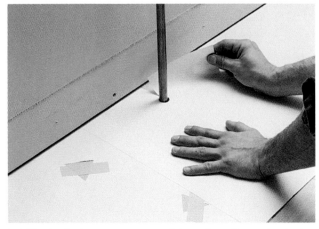

5 Fit the hole cutout around the pipe. Tape the hole template to adjoining sheets.

6 When completed, roll or loosely fold the paper template for carrying.

How to Install Perimeter-bond Sheet Vinyl

1 Unroll the flooring on any large, flat, clean surface. To prevent wrinkles, sheet vinyl comes from the manufacturer rolled with the pattern side out. Unroll the sheet and turn it pattern-side up for marking.

2 For two-piece installations, overlap the edges of sheets by at least 2". Plan seams to fall along the pattern lines or simulated grout joints. Align the sheets so that the pattern matches, then tape the sheets together with duct tape.

3 Position the paper template over the sheet vinyl, and tape it into place. Trace the outline of the template onto the flooring with a nonpermanent, felt-tipped pen.

4 Remove the template. Cut the sheet vinyl with a sharp linoleum knife, or a utility knife with a new sharp blade. Use a straightedge as a guide for making longer cuts.

5 Cut holes for pipes and other permanent obstructions. Then cut a slit from the hole to the nearest edge of the flooring. Make slits along pattern lines, if possible.

6 Roll up flooring loosely and transfer it to the installation area. Do not fold flooring. Unroll and position the sheet vinyl carefully. Slide the edges beneath undercut door casings.

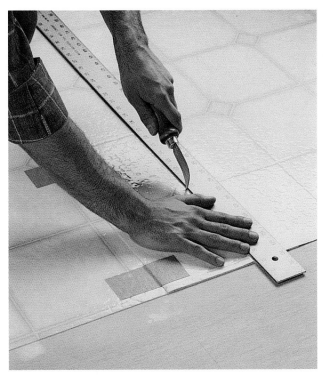

7 Cut seams for two-piece installations, using a straightedge as a guide. Hold the straightedge tightly against the flooring, and cut along the pattern lines through both pieces of vinyl flooring.

8 Remove both pieces of scrap flooring. The pattern should now run continuously across the adjoining sheets of flooring.

(continued next page)

9 Fold back the edges of both sheets and apply a 3" band of multipurpose flooring adhesive to the underlayment or old flooring, using a wallboard knife or ¼" notched trowel.

10 Lay seam edges one at a time into the adhesive. Make sure the seam is tight, pressing gaps together with your fingers, if needed. Roll the seam edges with a J-roller or wallpaper seam roller.

11 Apply flooring adhesive underneath flooring cuts at pipes or posts and around the entire perimeter of the room. Roll the flooring with the roller to ensure good contact with the adhesive.

12 If applying flooring over a wood underlayment, fasten the outer edges of the sheet to the floor with ⅜" staples driven every 3". Make sure the staples will be covered by the wall base molding.

How to Install Full-spread Sheet Vinyl

1 Cut the sheet vinyl using the techniques described on pages 72 and 73 (steps 1 to 5), then lay the sheet vinyl into position, sliding the edges underneath door casings.

2 Pull back half of the flooring, then apply a layer of flooring adhesive over the underlayment or old flooring, using a ¼" notched trowel. Lay the flooring back onto the adhesive.

3 Roll the floor with a floor roller, moving toward the edges of the sheet. The roller creates a stronger bond and eliminates air bubbles. Fold over the unbonded section of flooring, apply adhesive, then lay and roll the flooring. Wipe up any adhesive that oozes up around the edges of the vinyl, using a damp rag.

4 Measure and cut metal threshold bars to fit across doorways, then position each bar over the edge of the vinyl flooring and nail it in place.

Installing Resilient Tile

The key to a great-looking resilient tile installation is carefully positioning the layout lines. Once the layout lines are established, the actual installation of the tile is relatively easy, especially if you are using self-adhesive tile. Before committing to any layout, however, be sure to dry-fit the tiles to identify potential problems.

Tiles with an obvious grain pattern can be laid so the grain of each tile is oriented identically throughout the installation. Or, you can use the quarter-turn method, in which each tile is laid with its pattern grain running perpendicular to that of adjacent tiles.

Everything You Need:

Tools: basic hand tools, $\frac{1}{16}$" notched trowel (for dry-back tile).

Materials: resilient tile, flooring adhesive (for dry-back tile).

When installing self-adhesive resilient tile, install all full tiles in each layout quadrant first, then cut and install all partial tiles.

Tips for Installing Resilient Tile

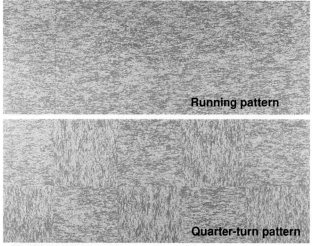

Running pattern

Quarter-turn pattern

Check for noticeable directional features, like the grain of the vinyl particles. You can choose to set the tile in a running pattern, so the directional feature runs in the same direction (top), or you can set the tiles in a checkerboard pattern, called the quarter-turn method (bottom).

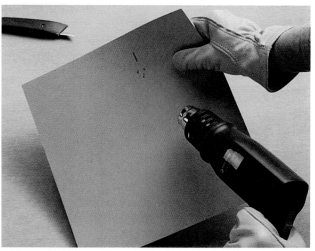

Make curved cuts in thick, rigid resilient tile by heating the back of the tile with a heat gun first, then cutting it while it is still warm.

How to Establish Perpendicular Reference Lines for a Tile Installation

1 Position a reference line (X) by measuring opposite sides of the room and marking the center of each side. Snap a chalk line between these marks.

2 Measure and mark the centerpoint of the chalk line. From this point, use a framing square to establish a second line perpendicular to the first. Snap a second reference line (Y) across the room.

3 Check for squareness using the "3-4-5 triangle" method. Measure and mark one reference line 3 ft. from the centerpoint on line X. Measure and mark the other reference line 4 ft. from the centerpoint on line Y. Measure the distance between the marks. If reference lines are perpendicular, the distance will measure exactly 5 ft. If not, adjust the reference lines until they are exactly perpendicular to one another.

How to Establish Tile Layout Lines

1 Snap perpendicular reference lines (X, Y) with a chalk line (see previous page). Dry-fit tiles along one perpendicular layout line (Y). If necessary, you can shift the layout one way or the other to make the layout visually symmetrical or to reduce the number of tiles that need to be cut.

2 If you have shifted the tile layout, create a new line that is parallel to reference line X and runs through a tile joint near the original line. This new line (X') will be one of the layout lines you will use when installing the tile. NOTE: To avoid confusion, use a different-colored chalk to distinguish between the original reference line and the new layout line.

3 Dry-fit tiles along the new layout line (X'). If necessary, adjust the layout, as in steps 1 and 2.

4 If you have adjusted the layout along line X', measure and mark a new layout line (Y') that is parallel to the reference line (Y) and runs through one of the tile joints. This new line will form the second layout line you will use during the installation.

How to Install Self-adhesive Resilient Tiles

1 Draw reference and layout lines (previous page), then peel off the paper backing and install the first tile in one of the corners formed by the intersecting layout lines. Lay three or more tiles along each layout line in the quadrant. Rub the entire surface of each tile to bond the adhesive to the floor underlayment.

2 Begin installing tiles in the interior area of the quadrant, making sure to keep the joints between tiles tight.

NOTE: Cut tile shown inverted for clarity; tiles should be faceup for marking.

3 Finish setting full-size tiles in the first quadrant, then set the full-size tiles in an adjacent quadrant. Set the tiles along the layout lines first, then fill in the interior tiles.

4 Cut tiles to fit against the walls. First, lay the tile to be cut (A) on top of the last full tile you installed. Position a ⅛"-thick spacer against the wall, then set a marker tile (B) on top of the tile to be cut. The uncovered portion of the tile to be cut will be the part you install. Trace along the edge of the marker tile to draw a cutting line.

(continued next page)

TIP: To mark tiles for cutting around outside corners, first make a cardboard template to match the space, with a ⅛" gap along the walls. After cutting the template, check to make sure it fits. Place the template on a tile, and trace its outline.

5 Cut the tile to fit, using a straightedge and a utility knife. Hold the straightedge securely against cutting lines to ensure a straight cut.

OPTION: To score and cut thick vinyl tiles (and ceramic tiles), use a tile cutter (page 85).

6 Install cut tiles next to the walls. TIP: For efficiency, you can precut all tiles, but first measure the distance between the wall and installed tiles at various points to make sure the variation does not exceed ½".

7 Continue installing tile in the remaining working quadrants until the room is completely covered. Check the entire floor, and if you find loose areas, press down on the tiles to bond them to the underlayment. Install metal threshold bars at project borders where the new floor joins another floor covering (page 75).

How to Install Dry-back Tile

1 Begin applying adhesive around the intersection of the layout lines, using a trowel with ¹⁄₁₆" V-shaped notches. Hold the trowel at a 45° angle, and spread adhesive evenly over the surface.

2 Spread adhesive over most of the installation area, covering three quadrants. Allow the adhesive to set according to manufacturer's instructions, then begin to install the tile at the intersection of the layout lines. (You can kneel on installed tiles to lay additional tiles.) When one quadrant is completely tiled, spread adhesive over the remaining quadrants, then finish setting the tile.

Ceramic Tile

Ceramic tile includes a wide variety of hard flooring products made from molded clay. Although there are significant differences among the various types, they are all installed using cement-based mortar as an adhesive and grout to fill the gaps between tiles. These same techniques can be used to install tiles cut from natural stone, like granite and marble.

Tile is the hardest of all flooring materials. With few exceptions, it is also the most expensive. But its durability makes it well worth the extra cost.

To ensure a long-lasting tile installation, the underlayment must be solid. Cementboard (or the thinner fiber/cementboard) is the best underlayment, since it has excellent stability and resists moisture. However, in rooms where moisture is not a factor, plywood is an adequate underlayment, and is considerably cheaper.

Many ceramic tiles have a glazed surface that protects the porous clay from staining. Unglazed ceramic tile should be protected with a sealer after it is installed. Grout sealers will prevent grout joints from trapping dirt and becoming discolored.

This section shows:
• Tools & Materials (pages 84 to 85)
• Cutting Tile (pages 86 to 87)
• Installing Ceramic Tile (pages 88 to 95)

Ceramic tiles include several categories of products that are molded from clay, then baked in a kiln. *Glazed ceramic tile* is coated with a colored glaze after it is baked, then is fired again to produce a hard surface layer, which is clearly visible when the tile is viewed along the edges. *Quarry tile* is an unglazed, porous tile that is typically softer and thicker than

glazed tiles. *Porcelain mosaic tile* is extremely dense and hard, and is naturally water-resistant. Like quarry tiles, porcelain tiles have the same color throughout their thickness when viewed along the edges. Porcelain tiles are often sold in mosaic sheets with a fiber or paper backing.

Natural-stone tiles are cut from stone extracted from quarries around the world. They are easily identified by visible saw marks at the edges and by their mineral veins or spots. Granite and marble tiles are generally sold with polished and sealed surfaces. Slate tiles are

formed by cleaving the stone along natural faults, rather than by machine-cutting, giving the tiles an appealing, textured look. Stone tile can be prohibitively expensive for large installations, but can be used economically as an accent in highly visible areas.

Thin-set mortar is a fine-grained cement product used to bond floor tile to underlayment. It is prepared by adding liquid a little at a time to the dry materials and stirring the mixture to achieve a creamy consistency. Some mortars include a latex additive in the dry mix, but with others you will need to add liquid latex additive when you prepare the mortar.

Tools & Materials

The tools required to cut tiles and to apply mortar and grout are generally small and fairly inexpensive.

Materials needed for a tile installation include: adhesive thin-set mortar, used to fasten the tiles to the underlayment; grout, used to fill the joints between tiles; and sealers, used to protect the tile surface and grout lines. Make sure to use the materials recommended by the tile manufacturer.

Trim and finishing materials for tile installations include base-trim tiles (A) which fit around the room perimeter, and bullnose tiles (B) used at doorways and other transition areas. Doorway thresholds (C) are made from synthetic materials as well as natural materials, such as marble, and come in thicknesses ranging from ¼" to ¾" to match different floor levels.

Tiling tools include adhesive-spreading tools, cutting tools, and grouting tools. Notched trowels (A) for spreading mortar come with notches of varying sizes and shapes; the size of the notch should be proportional to the size of the tile being installed. Cutting tools include a tile cutter (B), tile nippers (C), hand-held tile cutter (D), and jig saw with tungsten-carbide blade (E). Grouting tools include a grout float (F), grout sponge (G), buff rag (H), and foam brush (I). Other tiling tools include spacers (J), available in different sizes to create grout joints of varying widths; needle-nose pliers (K) for removing spacers; rubber mallet (L) for setting tiles into mortar; and caulk gun (M).

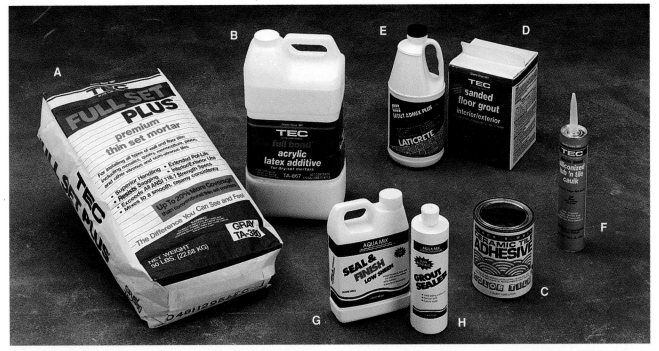

Tile materials include adhesives, grouts, and sealers. Thin-set mortar (A), the most common floor-tile adhesive, is often strengthened with latex mortar additive (B). Use wall-tile adhesive (C) for installing base-trim tile. Floor grout (D), is used to fill gaps between tiles; it is available in pretinted colors to match your tile. Grout can be made more resilient and durable with grout additive (E). Tile caulk (F) should be used in place of grout where tile meets another surface, like a bathtub. Porous tile sealer (G) and grout sealer (H) ward off stains and make maintenance easier.

Tile saws—also called wet saws because they use water to cool blades and tiles—are used primarily for cutting natural-stone tiles. They are also useful for quickly cutting notches in all kinds of hard tile. Wet saws are available for rent at tile dealers and rental shops.

Cutting Tile

Cutting tile accurately takes some practice and patience, but can be done effectively by do-it-yourselfers with the right tools.

Most cutting can be done with a basic tile cutter, such as the one shown on the opposite page. Tile cutters come in various configurations; each operates a little differently, though they all score and snap tile. Tile stores will often lend cutters to customers.

Other hand-held cutting tools are used to make small cuts or curved cuts.

Everything You Need:

Tools: wet saw, tile cutter, hand-held tile cutter, nippers, jig saw with tungsten-carbide blade.

Tips for Making Special Cuts

To make square notches, clamp the tile down on a worktable, then use a jig saw with a tungsten-carbide blade to make the cuts. If you need to cut many notches, a wet saw is more efficient.

To cut mosaic tiles, use a tile cutter to score tiles in the row where the cut will occur. Cut away excess strips of mosaics from the sheet, using a utility knife, then use a hand-held tile cutter to snap tiles one at a time. NOTE: Use tile nippers to cut narrow portions of tiles after scoring.

How to Make Straight Cuts in Ceramic Tile

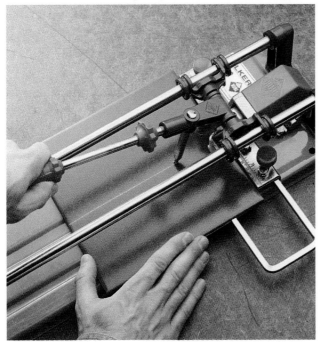

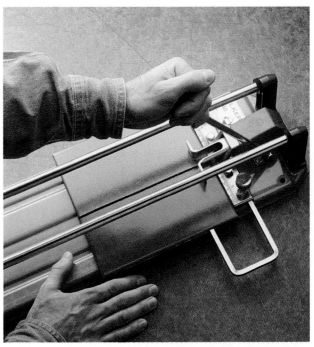

1 Mark a cutting line on the tile with a pencil, then place the tile in the cutter so the tile-cutting wheel is directly over the line. Pressing down firmly on the wheel handle, run the wheel across the tile to score the surface.

2 Snap the tile along the scored line, as directed by the tool manufacturer. Usually, snapping the tile is accomplished by depressing a lever on the tile cutter.

How to Make Curved Cuts with Tile Nippers

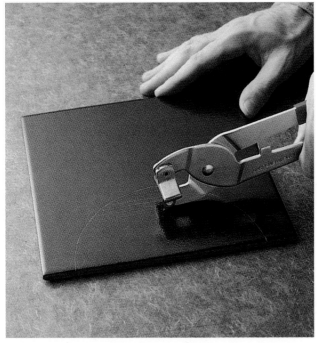

1 Mark a cutting line on the tile face, then use the scoring wheel of a hand-held tile cutter to score the cut line. Make several parallel scores, not more than ¼" apart, in the waste portion of the tile.

2 Use tile nippers to gradually remove the scored portion of the tile. TIP: To cut circular holes in the middle of a tile (step 10, page 91), first score and cut the tile so it divides the hole in two, using the straight-cut method, then use the curved-cut method to remove waste material from each half of the hole.

Installing Ceramic Tile

Ceramic tile installations start with the same steps as resilient tile projects: snapping perpendicular layout lines and dry-fitting tiles to ensure the best placement. These steps are shown on pages 76 to 78.

When you start setting tiles in thin-set mortar, work in small sections at a time so the mortar does not dry before the tiles are set. Also, plan your installation to avoid kneeling on set tiles.

Everything You Need:

Tools: basic hand tools, rubber mallet, tile cutter, tile nippers, hand-held tile cutter, needlenose pliers, grout float, grout sponge, soft cloth, small paint brush.

Materials: thin-set mortar, tile, tile spacers, grout, grout sealer, tile caulk.

How to Install Ceramic Tile

1 Draw reference and layout lines (pages 76 to 78), then mix a batch of thin-set mortar (page 84). Spread thin-set mortar evenly against both reference lines of one quadrant, using a ¼" square-notched trowel. Use the edge of the trowel to create furrows in the mortar bed.

VARIATION: For large tiles or uneven natural stone, use a larger trowel with notches that are at least ½" deep.

2 Set the first tile in the corner of the quadrant where the reference lines intersect. TIP: When setting tiles that are 8" square or larger, twist each tile slightly as you set it into position.

3 Using a soft rubber mallet, gently rap the central area of each tile a few times to set it evenly into the mortar.

VARIATION: For mosaic sheets, use a ³/₁₆" V-notched trowel to spread mortar, and use a grout float to press the sheets into the mortar.

4 To ensure consistent spacing between tiles, place plastic tile spacers at corners of the set tile. NOTE: With mosaic sheets, use spacers equal to the gaps between tiles.

(continued next page)

5 Position and set adjacent tiles into mortar along the reference lines. Make sure tiles fit neatly against the spacers. NOTE: Spacers are only temporary; be sure to remove them before the mortar hardens.

6 To make sure adjacent tiles are level with one another, lay a straight piece of 2 × 4 across several tiles at once, and rap the 2 × 4 with a mallet.

7 Lay tile in the remaining area covered with mortar. Repeat steps 1 to 6, continuing to work in small sections, until you reach walls or fixtures.

8 Measure and mark tiles for cutting to fit against walls and into corners (pages 79 to 80). Cut tiles to fit (pages 86 to 87). Apply thin-set mortar directly to the back of the cut tiles instead of the floor, using the notched edge of the trowel to furrow the mortar.

9 Set cut pieces into position, and press down on them until they are level with adjacent tiles.

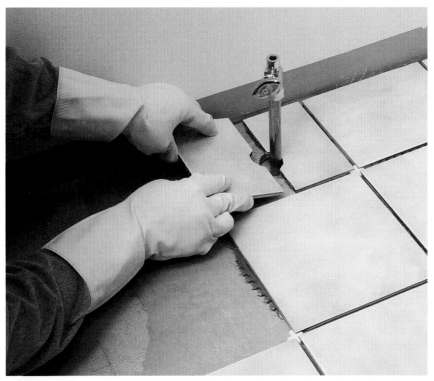

10 Measure, cut, and install tiles requiring notches or curves to fit around obstacles, such as exposed pipes.

11 Carefully remove spacers with needlenose pliers before the mortar hardens.

(continued next page)

12 Apply mortar and fill in tiles in remaining quadrants, completing one quadrant at a time before beginning the next. TIP: Before applying grout, inspect all of the tile joints and remove any high spots of mortar that could show through grout, using a utility knife or a grout knife.

13 Install threshold material in doorways. The most long-lasting thresholds are made from solid-surface mineral products. If the threshold is too long for the doorway, cut it to fit with a jig saw or circular saw and a tungsten-carbide blade. Set the threshold in thin-set mortar so the top is even with the tile. Keep the same space between the threshold as between tiles. Let the mortar cure for at least 24 hours.

14 Prepare a small batch of floor grout to fill tile joints. TIP: When mixing grout for porous tile, such as quarry or natural stone, use an additive with a release agent to prevent grout from bonding to the tile surfaces.

15 Starting in a corner, pour the grout over the tile. Use a rubber grout float to spread grout outward from the corner, pressing firmly on float to completely fill joints. For best results, tilt the float at a 60° angle to the floor and use a figure-eight motion.

16 Use the grout float to remove excess grout from the surface of the tile. Wipe diagonally across the joints, holding the float in a near-vertical position. Continue applying grout and wiping off excess until about 25 sq. ft. of the floor has been grouted.

17 Wipe a damp grout sponge diagonally over about 2 sq. ft. of the tile at a time to remove excess grout. Rinse the sponge in cool water between wipes. Wipe each area once only; repeated wiping can pull grout from the joints. Repeat steps 14 to 17 to apply grout to the rest of the floor.

18 Allow the grout to dry for about 4 hours, then use a soft cloth to buff the tile surface free of any remaining grout film.

(continued next page)

How to Install Ceramic Tile (continued)

19 Apply grout sealer to the grout lines, using a small sponge brush or sash brush. Avoid brushing sealer on the tile surfaces. Wipe up any excess sealer immediately.

VARIATION: Use a tile sealer to seal porous tile, such as quarry tile or any unglazed tile. Roll a thin coat of sealer (refer to manufacturer's instructions) over the tile and grout joints with a paint roller and extension handle.

How to Install Base-trim Tile

1 To give your new tiled floor a more professional look, install base-trim tiles at the bases of the walls. Start by dry-fitting the tiles to determine the best spacing (grout lines in base tile do not always align with grout lines in the floor tile). Use rounded "bullnose" tiles at outside corners, and mark tiles for cutting as needed.

2 Leaving a ⅛" expansion gap between tiles at corners, mark any contour cuts necessary to allow the coved edges to fit together. Use a jig saw with a tungsten-carbide blade to make curved cuts (see page 86).

3 Begin installing base-trim tiles at an inside corner. Use a notched trowel to apply wall adhesive to the back of the tile. Slip ⅛" spacers under each tile to create an expansion joint.

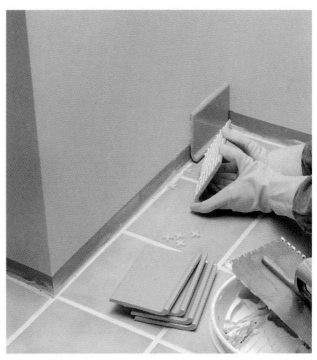

4 Press the tile into the adhesive. Continue setting tiles, using spacers to maintain ⅛" gaps between the tiles and an expansion joint between the tile and the floor.

5 At outside corners, use a double-bullnose tile on one side, to cover the edge of the adjoining tile.

6 After adhesive dries, grout the vertical joints between tiles, and apply grout along the tops of the tiles to make a continuous grout line. After grout cures, fill the expansion joint at the bottom of the tiles with caulk.

Installing manufactured wood flooring materials is a quicker, easier process than laying traditional solid hardwood. The hardwood veneer product shown here is edge-glued, using ordinary wood glue.

Hardwood Flooring

Hardwood flooring has undeniable appeal, but installing traditional solid hardwood planks is an expensive, difficult, and time-consuming job that few do-it-yourselfers are willing to attempt. However, many manufactured wood flooring products, designed for do-it-yourself installation, are now available. These materials offer the virtues of solid hardwood—strength; durability; attractive, warm appearance—but are easier to install.

These composite products come already stained and sealed with a protective coating. Like their solid hardwood counterparts, manu-

factured products have tongue-and-groove construction that ensures a tight bond between pieces.

Laminated planks, including plastic laminated flooring, can be installed in one of two ways. Flooring installed on a thin layer of adhesive is a good choice for areas that get a lot of foot traffic. A floating floor, which rests on a thin foam padding, can be installed over a variety of surfaces. It is the ideal choice over concrete slabs susceptible to moisture, such as those in basements.

Parquet flooring is installed with flooring adhesive, using the same installation strategy used for installing resilient or ceramic tile (pages 76 to 78).

Wood Flooring Options

Manufactured wood flooring materials include: fiberboard surfaced with a synthetic laminate layer that mimics the look of wood grain (left), plywood topped with a thin hardwood veneer (center), and parquet tiles made of wood strips bonded together in a decorative pattern (right).

Solid hardwood flooring is more expensive and more difficult to install than manufactured wood flooring. If you want a solid hardwood floor, consider hiring a professional to install it.

Stripping and refinishing an existing solid hardwood floor will give you a surface that looks like new. For help doing this, see our Black & Decker® Home Improvement Library™: *Refinishing & Finishing Wood.*

Materials for Hardwood Flooring Installation

Foam backing for use under floating plank floors comes in several thicknesses. The thinner foam backing on the left is installed under synthetic laminate flooring; the thicker backing on the right is laid under plywood-backed flooring.

Adhesives used to install hardwood flooring include white glue for joining edges of floating plank flooring and latex adhesive for glue-down floors.

T-shaped hardwood threshold spans transitions between hardwood floors and other flooring of equal height. These products, available through hardwood flooring manufacturers, are glued in place.

Reducers are wood transitions used between hardwood flooring and an adjacent floor of lower height. One edge is grooved to fit the tongue on hardwood planks, and the other edge has a rounded bullnose. Reducers come in several thicknesses and styles for your particular needs.

How to Cut Hardwood Flooring

Ripcut hardwood planks from the back side to avoid splintering the top surface when cutting. Measure the distance from the wall to the edge of the last board installed, subtracting ½" to allow for an expansion gap. Transfer the measurement to the back of the flooring, and mark the cut with a chalk line (left).

When ripcutting hardwood flooring with a circular saw, place another piece of flooring next to the piece marked for cutting to provide a stable surface for the foot of the saw (right). Also, clamp a cutting guide to the planks at the correct distance from the cutting line to ensure a straight cut.

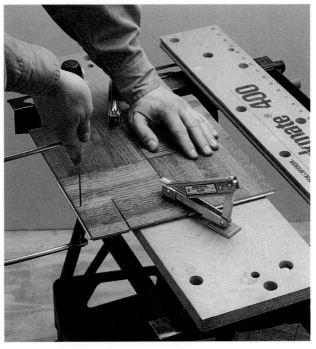

Crosscut hardwood planks on a power miter box, with the top surface of the planks facing up to prevent splintering.

Make notched or curved cuts in hardwood flooring with a coping saw or jig saw. If using a jig saw, the finished surface of the flooring should face down.

Installing Hardwood Floors

How you install hardwood floors will depend on the product you have chosen. Synthetic laminate flooring should be installed only using the "floating" technique, in which the flooring is glued edge to edge and installed over a foam backing. Parquet flooring should only be glued down over troweled-on adhesive. Follow the instructions for "Installing Resilient Tile" (pages 76 to 78). Plywood-backed hardwood flooring can be installed using either method.

Everything You Need:

Tools: basic hand tools, coping saw, circular saw, ⅛" notched trowel, tool bar, mallet, linoleum roller.

Materials: hardwood flooring, flooring adhesive, wood glue, cardboard, foam backing, masking tape.

How to Install Wood Strip Flooring Using Adhesive

1 To establish a straight layout line, snap a chalk line parallel to the longest wall, about 30" from the wall. Kneel in this space to begin flooring installation.

2 Apply flooring adhesive to the subfloor on the other side of the layout line with a notched trowel, according to the manufacturer's directions. Take care not to obscure the layout line with adhesive.

3 Apply wood glue to the grooved end of each piece as you install it, to help joints stay tight. Do not apply glue to long sides of boards.

4 Install the first row of flooring with the edge of the tongues directly over chalk line. Make sure end joints are tight, then wipe up any excess glue immediately. At walls, leave a ½" space to allow for expansion of the wood. This gap will be covered by the baseboard and base shoe.

5 For succeeding rows, insert the tongue into the groove of the preceding row, and pivot the flooring down into the adhesive. Gently slide the tongue-and-groove ends together. TIP: At walls, you can use a hammer and a hardwood flooring tool bar to draw together the joints on the last strip (inset).

(continued next page)

6 After you've installed three or four rows, use a mallet and a scrap of flooring to gently tap boards together, closing up the seams. All joints should fit tightly.

7 Use a cardboard template to fit boards in irregular areas. Cut cardboard to match the space, and allow for a ½" expansion gap next to the wall. Trace the template outline on a board, then cut it to fit, using a jig saw. Finish layering strips over the entire floor.

8 Bond the flooring by rolling with a heavy flooring roller. Roll the flooring within 3 hours of the adhesive application. (Rollers can be borrowed or rented from flooring distributors.)

How to Install a Floating Plank Floor

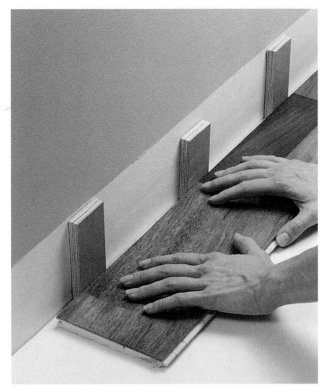

1 Roll out the appropriate foam backing (page 98) and cut it in strips to fit the room. Secure all seams with masking tape. Do not overlap seams.

2 Begin installation at the longest wall. Use ½" spacers to provide a gap for expansion of the flooring.

3 Join planks by applying wood glue to the grooves of the planks. Complete the installation, using the same method used for glue-down flooring (steps 5 to 7). Be sure to glue end joints as well.

Cabinets

Cabinets determine how a kitchen looks and functions. Cabinets should provide adequate storage, and have a pleasing appearing that harmonizes with other elements in the kitchen and home.

Paint existing cabinets to give your entire kitchen new life at a minimum cost. Wood, metal, and previously painted cabinets may be painted any color. Do not paint plastic laminate.

Reface cabinets to create a dramatic change in style. Refacing kits include new cabinet doors, drawer fronts, and matching veneer for covering

face frames and cabinet ends. All types of cabinets can be refaced.

Install new cabinets to transform a kitchen completely. New cabinets come in a wide range of styles of accessories that can increase storage efficiency.

Several companies make modular cabinets designed especially for do-it-yourself installations. Modular cabinets have finished end panels on both sides, and can be arranged to fit any kitchen layout.

Painting Cabinets

Paint cabinets to renew your kitchen quickly and inexpensively. Cabinets receive heavy use and are frequently scrubbed, so paint them with a heavy-duty gloss enamel. Enamel paint is more durable than flat wall paint. Sand surfaces lightly between coats.

Use natural bristle paint brushes with alkyd paints, synthetic bristle brushes with latex.

Varnished cabinets can be painted if the surface is properly prepared. Use liquid deglosser to dull the shine, then prime all surfaces. Alkyd paints work best for painting varnished cabinets.

Specialty tools & supplies include: work light (A), paint pan (B), paint remover (C), primer/sealer (D), tapered sash brush (E), trim brush (F), scraper (G), sandpaper (H), paint rollers (I).

Everything You Need:

Basic Hand Tools: screwdriver.
Basic Materials: gloss enamel paint.
Specialty Tools & Supplies: photo right.

How to Paint Cabinets

1 Wash cabinets with mild detergent. Scrape loose paint. Sand all surfaces. Wipe away sanding dust and prime all bare wood with sealer.

2 Paint interiors first, in this order: 1) back walls, 2) tops, 3) sides, 4) bottoms. Paint bottoms, tops, and edges of shelves last.

3 Paint both sides of doors beginning with inner surfaces. With panel doors, paint in this order: 1) recessed panels, 2) horizontal rails, 3) vertical stiles.

Framed cabinets have openings that are completely surrounded by face frames made of vertical stiles and horizontal rails. They give kitchens a traditional look.

Frameless cabinets, sometimes called "European-style," are more contemporary. Because they have no face frames, frameless cabinets offer slightly more storage space than framed cabinets.

Hinges on framed cabinets are screwed directly to the face frames. Better cabinets have adjustable hinges that allow door realignment.

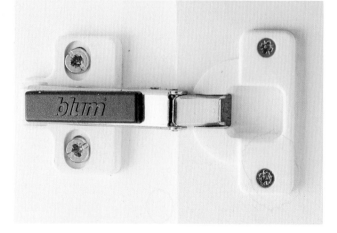

Hinges on frameless cabinets are screwed directly to the inside of the cabinet, eliminating the need for face frames. Hinges are hidden, providing a cleaner look.

Selecting New Cabinets

Kitchen cabinets come in a wide array of shapes and finishes, but their basic construction is similar. Different styles of doors, drawer fronts, and hardware give cabinets their individual character and personality.

Framed cabinets have cabinet openings that are completely surrounded by face frames, and door hinges are attached directly to the frames. Framed cabinets typically have a traditional look.

Frameless cabinets (also called "European-style") have no face frames. Special "invisible" hinges attach to the inside walls of the cabinet. The doors and drawers on frameless cabinets cover the entire unit, providing contemporary styling and slightly more storage space.

Modular cabinets have finished panels on both sides, and can be arranged in a variety of ways to fit any kitchen layout. Modular cabinet doors can be reversed to open from either left or right. They are especially suited to do-it-yourself installations.

Specification booklet lists all dimensions of cabinets and trim pieces. Draw a kitchen floor plan on graph paper, and use catalog when sketching cabinet layout.

Modular cabinets have finished panels on both sides, and can be arranged in a variety of ways to fit any kitchen layout. Modular cabinet doors can be reversed to open from either left or right. They are especially suited to do-it-yourself installations.

All cabinet manufacturers offer a selection of specialty cabinets, storage accessories, and decorative trim. Check manufacturers' product-line catalogs for complete listings of available cabinets and accessories.

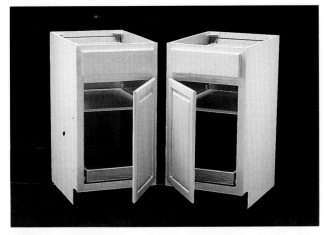

Modular cabinets have finished panels on both sides. Doors can be reversed to open from either left or right. Modular cabinets can be arranged to fit any kitchen layout.

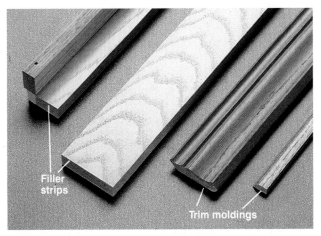

Filler strips

Trim moldings

Prefinished trim pieces match the finish of modular cabinets. Filler strips are used in spaces between cabinets, or between a cabinet and wall or appliance. Small trim moldings cover gaps between cabinet edges and walls.

Removing Trim & Old Cabinets

How to Remove Trim & Old Cabinets

1 Remove any vinyl base trim. Work a pry bar or putty knife underneath and peel off the vinyl. Remove trim moldings at edges and tops of cabinets with a flat pry bar.

2 Remove baseboard moldings with a pry bar. Protect wall surfaces with a scrap of wood. Remove countertop (see page 121).

3 Remove doors and drawers to make it easier to get at interior spaces. At back of cabinets, remove any screws holding cabinet to wall.

4 Detach individual cabinets by removing screws that hold face frames together. Remove valances. Some are attached to cabinets with screws, others are nailed and must be pried loose.

Preparing for New Cabinets

Installing new cabinets is easiest if the kitchen is completely empty. Disconnect the plumbing and wiring, and temporarily remove the appliances. To remove old cabinets, see page 95. If the new kitchen requires plumbing or electrical changes, now is the time to have this work done. If the kitchen flooring is to be replaced, finish it before beginning layout and installation of cabinets.

Cabinets must be installed plumb and level. Using a level as a guide, draw reference lines on the walls to indicate cabinet location. If the kitchen floor is uneven, find the highest point of the floor area that will be covered by base cabinets. Measure up from this point to draw reference lines.

Sanded high area

Stud finder

Filled-in low area

Stud locations

1 x 3 ledger

Reference line

1 Find high and low spots on wall surfaces, using a long, straight 2 × 4. Sand down any high spots.

2 Fill in low spots of wall. Apply wallboard taping compound with a trowel. Let dry, and sand lightly.

3 Locate and mark wall studs, using an electronic stud finder. Cabinets will be hung by driving screws into the studs through the back of the cabinets.

High point

4 Find high point along the floor area that will be covered by base cabinets. Place a level on a long, straight 2 × 4, and move board across floor to determine if floor is uneven. Mark wall at the high point.

5 Measure up 34½" from the high-point mark. Use a level to mark a reference line on walls. Base cabinets will be installed with top edges flush against this line.

6 Measure up 84" from the high-point mark and draw a second reference line. Wall cabinets will be installed with top edges flush against this line.

7 Measure down 30" from wall-cabinet reference line and draw another level line where bottom of cabinets will be. Temporary ledgers will be installed against this line.

8 Install 1 × 3 temporary ledgers with top edge flush against the reference line. Attach ledgers with 2½" wallboard screws driven into every other wall stud. Mark stud locations on ledgers. Cabinets will rest temporarily on ledgers during installation.

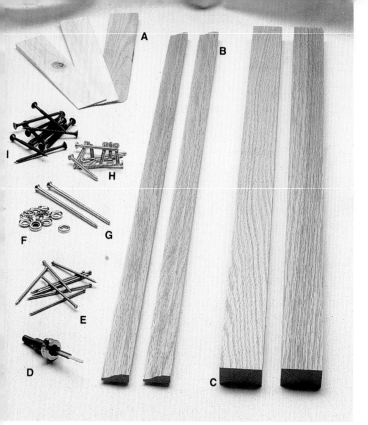

Specialty tools & supplies include: wood shims (A), trim moldings (B), filler strips (C), No. 9 counterbore drill bit (D), 6d finish nails (E), finish washers (F), No. 10 gauge 4" wood screws (G), No. 8 gauge 2½" sheetmetal screws (H), 3" wallboard screws (I).

Installing Cabinets

Cabinets must be firmly anchored to wall studs, and must be exactly plumb and level, so that the doors and drawers operate smoothly. Number each cabinet and mark its position on the wall. Remove the cabinet doors and drawers, and number them so they can be easily replaced after the cabinets are installed.

Begin with the corner cabinets, making sure they are installed plumb and level. Adjacent cabinets are easily aligned once the corner cabinets have been correctly positioned.

Everything You Need:

Basic Hand Tools: handscrew clamps, level, hammer, utility knife, nail set, stepladder.

Basic Power Tools: drill with ³⁄₁₆" twist bit, cordless screwdriver, jig saw with wood-cutting blade.

Basic Materials: cabinets, trim molding, toe-kick molding, filler strips, valance.

Specialty Tools & Supplies: photo, right.

How to Fit Blind Corner Cabinet

Before installation, test-fit corner and adjoining cabinets to make sure doors and handles do not interfere with each other. If necessary, increase the clearance by pulling the blind cabinet away from side wall by no more than 4". To maintain even spacing between edges of doors and cabinet corner (A, B), cut a filler strip and attach it to the adjoining cabinet. Measure distance (C) as a reference when positioning blind cabinet against wall.

How to Install Wall Cabinets

1 Position corner cabinet on ledger. Drill ³⁄₁₆" pilot holes into studs through hanging strips at rear of cabinet. Attach to wall with 2½" sheetmetal screws. Do not tighten fully until all cabinets are hung.

2 Attach filler strip to adjoining cabinet, if needed (see page opposite). Clamp filler in place, and drill pilot holes through cabinet face frame near hinge locations, using a counterbore bit. Attach filler to cabinet with 2½" sheetmetal screws.

3 Position adjoining cabinet on ledger, tight against blind corner cabinet. Check face frame for plumb. Drill ³⁄₁₆" pilot holes into wall studs through hanging strips in rear of cabinet. Attach cabinet with 2½" sheetmetal screws. Do not tighten wall screws fully until all cabinets are hung.

4 Clamp corner cabinet and adjoining cabinet together at the top and bottom. Handscrew clamps will not damage wood face frames.

(continued next page)

5 Attach blind corner cabinet to adjoining cabinet. From inside corner cabinet, drill pilot holes through face frame. Join cabinets with sheetmetal screws.

6 Position and attach each additional cabinet. Clamp frames together, and drill counterbored pilot holes through side of face frame. Join cabinets with sheetmetal screws. Drill ³⁄₁₆" pilot holes in hanging strips, and attach cabinet to studs with sheetmetal screws.

Join frameless cabinets with No. 8 gauge 1¼" wood screws and finish washers. Each pair of cabinets should be joined by at least four screws.

7 Fill small spaces between a cabinet and a wall or appliance with a filler strip. Cut filler to fit space, then wedge filler into place with wood shims. Drill counterbored pilot holes through side of cabinet face frame, and attach filler with sheetmetal screws.

8 Remove temporary ledger. Check cabinet run for plumb, and adjust if necessary by placing wood shims behind cabinet, near stud locations. Tighten wall screws completely. Cut off shims with utility knife.

9 Use trim moldings to cover any gaps between cabinets and walls. Stain moldings to match cabinet finish.

10 Attach decorative valance above sink. Clamp valance to edge of cabinet frames, and drill counterbored pilot holes through cabinet frames into end of valance. Attach with sheetmetal screws.

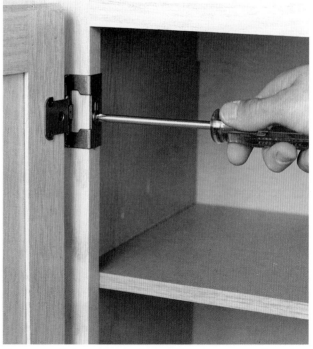

11 Install the cabinet doors. If necessary, adjust the hinges so that the doors are straight and plumb.

How to Install Base Cabinets

1 Begin installation with corner cabinet. Position cabinet so that top is flush with reference line. Make sure cabinet is plumb and level. If necessary, adjust by driving wood shims under cabinet base. Be careful not to damage flooring. Drill ³/₁₆'' pilot holes through hanging strip into wall studs. Attach cabinets loosely to wall with sheetmetal screws.

2 Attach filler strip to adjoining cabinet, if necessary (page 113). Clamp filler in place, and drill counter-bored pilot holes through side of face frame. Attach filler with sheetmetal screws.

3 Clamp adjoining cabinet to corner cabinet. Make sure cabinet is plumb, then drill counterbored pilot holes through corner-cabinet face frame into filler strip (page 114, step 5). Join cabinets with sheetmetal screws. Drill ³/₁₆" pilot holes through hanging strips into wall studs. Attach cabinets loosely with sheetmetal screws.

4 Use a jig saw to cut any cabinet openings needed for plumbing, wiring, or heating ducts.

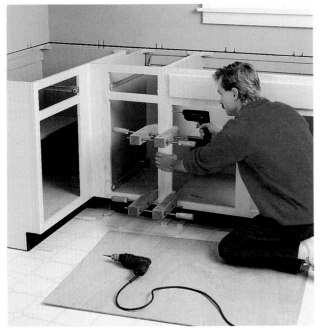

5 Position and attach additional cabinets, making sure frames are aligned. Clamp cabinets together, then drill counterbored pilot holes through side of face frame. Join cabinets with sheetmetal screws. Frameless cabinets are joined with No. 8 gauge 1¼" wood screws and finish washers (page 114).

6 Make sure all cabinets are level. If necessary, adjust by driving wood shims underneath cabinets. Place wood shims behind cabinets near stud locations wherever there is a gap. Tighten wall screws. Cut off shims with utility knife.

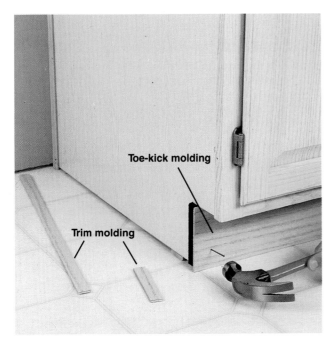

Toe-kick molding

Trim molding

7 Use trim moldings to cover gaps between the cabinets and the wall or floor. Toe-kick area is often covered with a strip of hardwood finished to match the cabinets.

8 If corner has void area not covered by cabinets, screw 1 × 3 cleats to wall, flush with reference line. Cleats will help support countertop.

How to Install a Ceiling-hung Cabinet to Joists

1 Cut a cardboard template to same size as top of wall cabinet. Use template to outline position of cabinet on ceiling. Mark position of the cabinet face frame on the outline.

2 Locate joists with stud finder. If joists run parallel to cabinet, install blocking between joists to hang cabinet (below). Measure joist positions and mark cabinet frame to indicate where to drive screws.

3 Have one or more helpers position cabinet against ceiling. Drill 3/16" pilot holes through top rails into ceiling joists. Attach cabinets with 4" wood screws and finish washers.

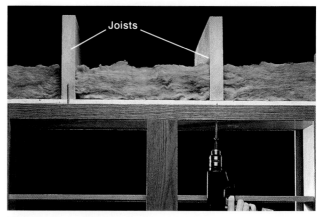

Shown in cutaway: Cabinet is attached to joists with wood screws and finish washers.

How to Attach a Ceiling-hung Cabinet to Blocking (joists must be accessible)

1 Drill reference holes through the ceiling at each corner of cabinet outline. From above ceiling, install 2 × 4 blocks between joists. Blocking can be toenailed, or end-nailed through joists.

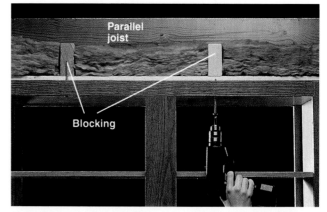

2 Measure distance between each block and the drilled reference holes. Mark cabinet frame to indicate where to drive anchoring screws. Drill pilot holes and attach cabinet to blocking with 4" wood screws and finish washers, as shown in cutaway (above).

118

How to Install a Base Island Cabinet

1 Set the base cabinet in the correct position, and lightly trace the cabinet outline on the flooring. Remove cabinet.

2 Attach L-shaped 2 × 4 cleats to floor at opposite corners of cabinet outline. Allow for thickness of cabinet walls by positioning cleats ¾" inside cabinet outline. Attach cleat to floor with 3" wallboard screws.

3 Lower the base cabinet over the cleats. Check cabinet for level, and shim under the base if necessary.

4 Attach the cabinet to the floor cleats using 6d finish nails. Drill pilot holes for nails, and recess nail heads with a nail set.

Custom laminate

Post-form

Ceramic tile

Solid surface

Countertops

Countertops provide the main workspace in a kitchen, so they must be made from durable and easy-to-clean materials. Countertops add color, pattern, texture, and shape to kitchens, so choose a style that harmonizes with the other elements in the room.

Custom laminate countertops are built by gluing sheet laminates to particleboard. Laminates are available in hundreds of colors and patterns to match any kitchen decorating scheme. Special edge treatments can be added to customize a laminate countertop.

Post-form countertops are made of sheet laminates glued to particleboard, and come from the factory ready to install. Post-form countertops have pre-attached backsplashes and front edge treatments. They are manufactured in a variety of colors and styles.

Ceramic tile is especially durable and creates a beautiful surface that resists spills and stains. Tile is available in a wide range of styles and prices, and creating a ceramic tile countertop is an excellent do-it-yourself project.

Solid-surface materials are increasing in popularity. Manufactured from acrylic or polyester resins mixed with additives and formed into sheets, they are available in a wide variety of colors and styles. Solid-surface materials are expensive, but they are extremely durable and easy to maintain. However, they must be installed by professionals.

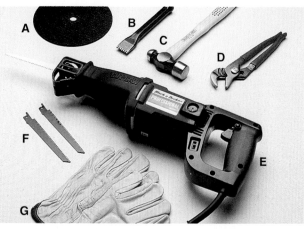

Specialty tools & supplies for removing countertops include: masonry-cutting ciruclar saw blade (A), masonry chisel (B), ball peen hammer (C), channel-type pliers (D), reciprocating saw (E) with coarse wood-cutting blade (F), work gloves (G).

How to Remove an Old Countertop

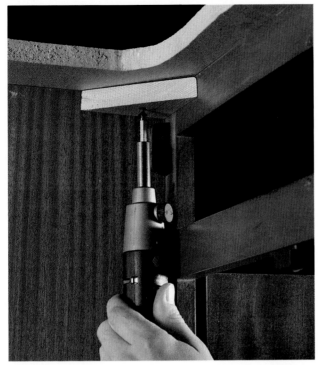

1 Turn off water at shutoff valves. Disconnect and remove plumbing fixtures and appliances. Remove any brackets or screws holding the countertop to the cabinets. Unscrew the take-up bolts on mitered countertops.

2 Use a utility knife to cut caulk beads along back-splash and edge of countertop. Remove any trim. Using a flat pry bar, try to lift countertop away from base cabinets.

3 If countertop cannot be pried up, use a reciprocating saw or jig saw with coarse wood-cutting blade to cut the countertop into pieces for removal. Be careful not to cut into base cabinets.

Ceramic tile: Wear eye protection. Chisel tile away from the base with a masonry chisel and ball peen hammer. A tile countertop that has a mortar bed can be cut into pieces with a circular saw and abrasive masonry-cutting blade.

Installing a
Post-form Countertop

Post-form laminate countertops come in stock lengths, and are cut to fit your kitchen space. Pre-mitered sections are available for two- or three-piece countertops that continue around corners. If the countertop has an exposed end, you will need an endcap kit that contains a preshaped strip of matching laminate.

For a precise fit, the backsplash must be trimmed to fit any unevenness in the back wall. This process is called scribing. Post-form countertops have a narrow strip of laminate on the backsplash for scribing.

Everything You Need:

Basic Hand Tools: tape measure, framing square, pencil, straightedge, C-clamps, hammer, level, caulk gun.

Basic Power Tools: jig saw, belt sander, drill and spade bit, cordless screwdriver.

Basic Materials: post-form countertop sections.

Specialty Tools & Supplies: photo, page opposite.

How to Install a Post-form Countertop

1 Measure span of base cabinets, from corner to outside edge of cabinet. Add 1'' for overhang if end will be exposed. If an end will butt against an appliance, subtract 1/16'' to prevent scratches.

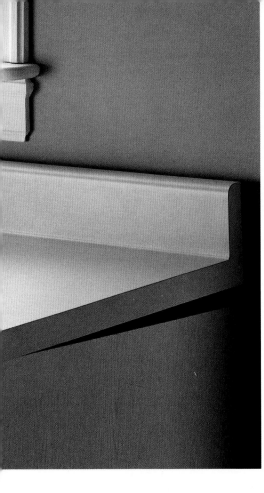

Specialty tools & supplies include: wood shims (A), take-up bolts (B), wallboard screws (C), wire brads (D), household iron (E), endcap laminate (F), endcap battens (G), silicone caulk (H), file (I), adjustable wrench (J), carpenter's glue (K),⸳ buildup blocks (L), scribing compass (M).

2 Use a framing square to mark a cutting line on the bottom surface of the countertop. Cut off the countertop with a jig saw, using a clamped straight-edge as a guide.

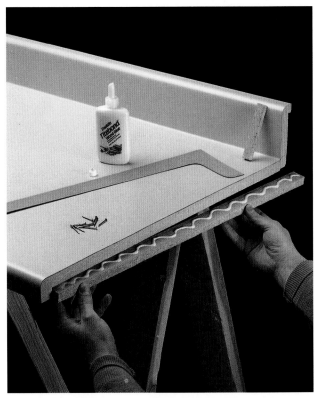

3 Attach battens from endcap kit to edge of counter-top, using carpenter's glue and small brads. Sand out any unevenness with belt sander.

(continued next page)

4 Hold endcap laminate against end, slightly over-lapping edges. Activate adhesive by pressing an iron set at medium heat against endcap. Cool with wet cloth, then file endcap laminate flush with edges.

5 Position countertop on base cabinets. Make sure front edge of countertop is parallel to cabinet face. Check countertop for level. Make sure that drawers and doors open and close freely. If needed, adjust countertop with wood shims.

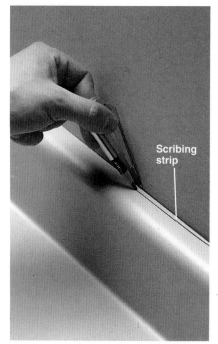

Scribing strip

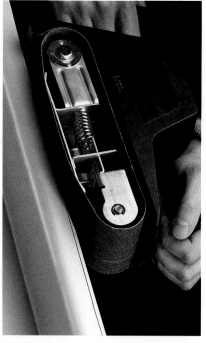

6 Because walls are usually un-even, use a compass to trace wall outline onto backsplash scrib-ing strip. Set compass arms to match widest gap, then move compass along length of the wall to transfer outline to scribing strip.

7 Remove countertop. Use belt sander to grind backsplash to scribe line.

8 Mark cutout for self-rimming sink. Position sink upside down on countertop and trace outline. Remove sink and draw cutting line 5/8" inside sink outline. To install sink, see page 144.

9 Mark cutout for cooktop or sink with frame. Position metal frame on countertop, and trace outline around edge of vertical flange. Remove frame. To install a framed cooktop or sink, see page 144.

10 Drill pilot hole just inside cutting line. Make cutouts with jig saw. Support cutout area from below so that falling cutout does not damage cabinet.

11 Apply a bead of silicone caulk on edges of mitered countertop sections. Force countertop pieces tightly together.

 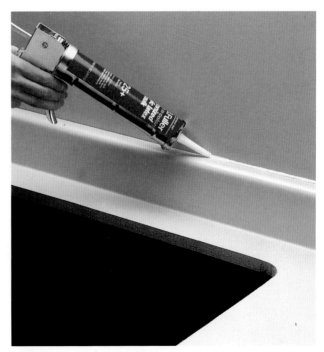

12 From underneath cabinet, install and tighten miter take-up bolts. Position countertop tightly against wall and fasten to cabinets by driving wallboard screws up through corner brackets into the countertop (page 137). Screws should be long enough to provide maximum holding power, but not long enough to puncture laminate surface.

13 Seal seam between backsplash and wall with silicone caulk. Smooth bead with a wet fingertip. Wipe away excess caulk.

Building a Custom Laminate Countertop

Build your own durable, beautiful countertop with plastic sheet laminates. Plastic laminates are available in hundreds of colors, styles, and textures. A countertop made with laminates can be tailored to fit any space.

Laminates are sold in 6-, 8-, 10-, or 12-foot lengths that are about $\frac{1}{20}$" thick. Laminate sheets range in width from 30" to 48". Most laminates are made by bonding a thin surface layer of colored plastic to a core of hardened resins. Another type of laminate has consistent color through the thickness of the sheet. Solid-color laminate countertops do not show dark lines at the trimmed edges, but they chip more easily than traditional laminates and must be handled carefully.

Choose nonflammable contact cement when building a countertop, and thoroughly ventilate your work area.

Everything You Need:

Basic Hand Tools: tape measure, framing square, pencil, straightedge, clamps, caulk gun.

Basic Power Tools: circular saw with combination blade, cordless screwdriver, belt sander, router.

Basic Materials: $\frac{3}{4}$" particleboard, sheet laminate.

Specialty Tools & Materials: photo, page opposite.

Laminate countertop: Countertop core is ¾" particleboard. Perimeter is built up with strips of particleboard screwed to the bottom of the core. For decorative edge treatments, hardwood strips can be attached to core.

Laminate pieces are bonded to the countertop with contact cement. Edges are trimmed and shaped with a router.

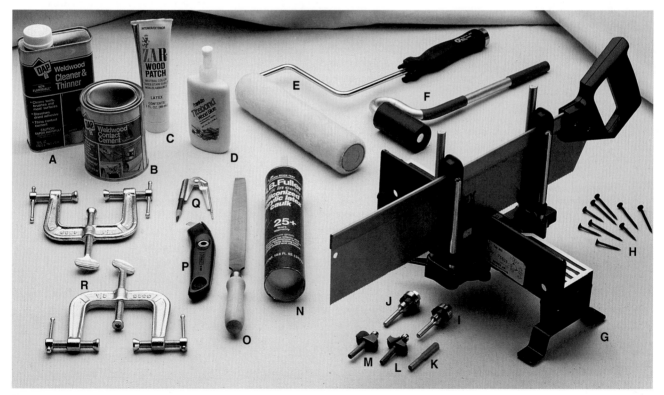

Specialty tools & supplies include: contact cement thinner (A), contact cement (B), latex wood patch (C), carpenter's glue (D), paint roller (E), J-roller (F), miter box (G), wallboard screws (H), flush-cutting router bit (I), 15° bevel-cutting router bit (J), straight router bit (K), corner rounding router bit (L), cove router bit (M), silicone caulk (N), file (O), scoring tool (P), scribing compass (Q), 3-way clamps (R).

How to Build a Custom Laminate Countertop

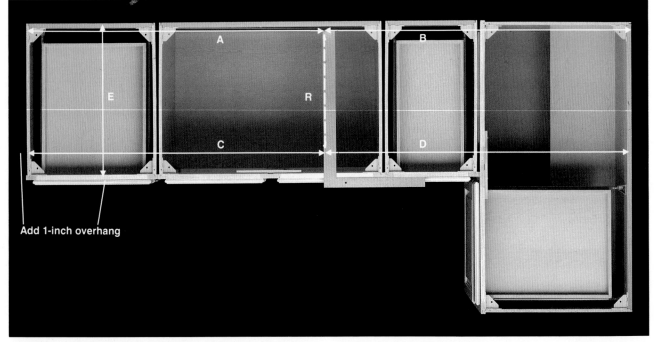

Add 1-inch overhang

1 Measure along tops of base cabinets to determine size of countertop. If wall corners are not square, use a framing square to establish a reference line (R) near middle of base cabinets, perpendicular to front of cabinets. Take four measurements (A, B, C, D) from reference line to cabinet ends. Allow for overhangs by adding 1" to the length for each exposed end, and 1" to the width (E). If an end butts against an appliance, subtract 1/16" from length to prevent scratching appliance.

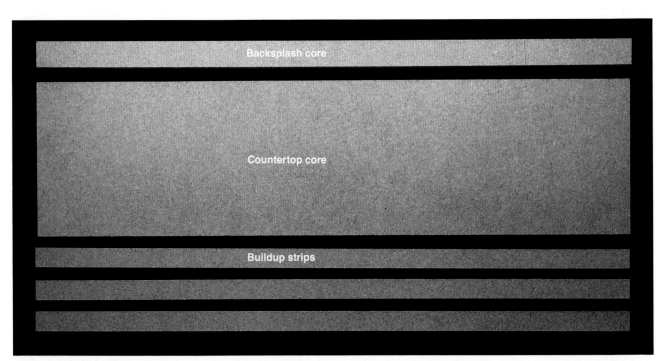

Backsplash core

Countertop core

Buildup strips

2 Transfer measurements from step 1, using a framing square to establish a reference line. Cut core to size using a circular saw with clamped straightedge as a guide. Cut 4" strips of particleboard for backsplash, and for joint support where sections of countertop core are butted together. Cut 3" strips for edge buildups.

128

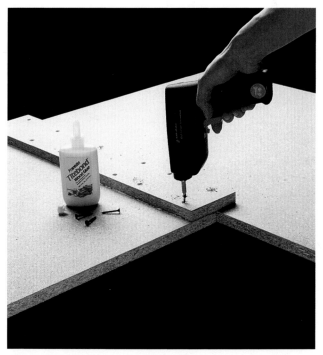

3 Join the countertop core pieces on the bottom side. Attach a 4" particle board joint support across the seam, using carpenter's glue and 1¼" wallboard screws.

4 Attach 3" edge buildup strips to bottom of countertop, using 1¼" wallboard screws. Fill any gaps on outside edges with latex wood patch, then sand edges with belt sander.

5 To determine the size of the laminate top, measure countertop core. For strength, laminate seams should run opposite to core seam. Add ½" trimming margin to both the length and width of each piece. Measure laminate needed for face and edges of backsplash, and for exposed edges of countertop core. Add ½" to each measurement.

6 Cut laminate by scoring and breaking it. Draw a cutting line, then etch along the line with a scoring tool. Use a straightedge as a guide. Two passes of scoring tool will help laminate break cleanly.

(continued next page)

7 Bend laminate toward the scored line until the sheet breaks cleanly. For better control on narrow pieces, clamp a straightedge along scored line before bending laminate. Wear gloves to avoid being cut by sharp edges.

8 Create tight-fitting seams with plastic laminate by using a router and a straight bit to trim edges that will butt together. Measure from cutting edge of the bit to edge of the router baseplate (A). Place laminate on scrap wood and align edges. To guide the router, clamp a straightedge on the laminate at distance A plus 1/4", parallel to laminate edge. Trim laminate.

9 Apply laminate to sides of countertop first. Using a paint roller, apply two coats of contact cement to edge of countertop and one coat to back of laminate. Let cement dry according to manufacturer's directions. Position laminate carefully, then press against edge of countertop. Bond with J-roller.

10 Use a router and flush-cutting bit to trim edge strip flush with top and bottom surfaces of countertop core. At edges where router cannot reach, trim excess laminate with a file. Apply laminate to remaining edges, and trim with router.

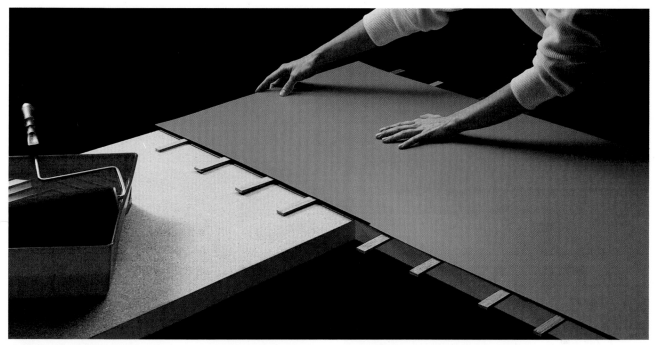

11 Test-fit laminate top on countertop core. Check that laminate overhangs all edges. At seam locations, draw a reference line on core where laminate edges will butt together. Remove laminate. Make sure all surfaces are free of dust, then apply one coat of contact cement to back of laminate and two coats to core. Place spacers made of 1/4"-thick scrap wood at 6" intervals across countertop core. Because contact cement bonds instantly, spacers allow laminate to be positioned accurately over core without bonding. Align laminate with seam reference line. Beginning at one end, remove spacers and press laminate to countertop core.

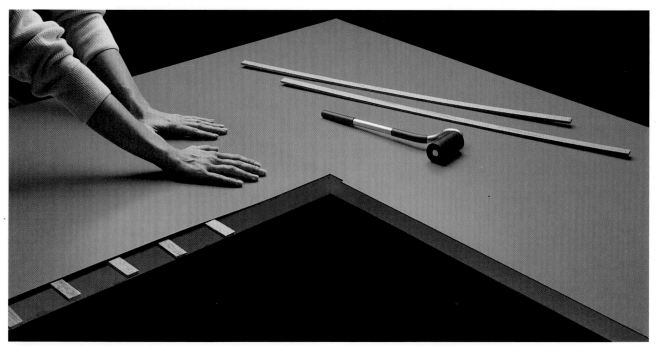

12 Apply contact cement to remaining core and next piece of laminate. Let cement dry, then position laminate on spacers, and carefully align butt seam. Beginning at seam edge, remove spacers and press laminate to countertop core.

(continued next page)

13 Roll entire surface with J-roller to bond laminate to core. Clean off any excess contact cement with a soft cloth and contact cement thinner.

14 Remove excess laminate with a router and flush-cutting bit. At edges where router cannot reach, trim excess laminate with a file. Countertop is now ready for final trimming with bevel-cutting bit.

15 Finish-trim the edges with router and 15° bevel-cutting bit. Set bit depth so that the bevel edge is cut only on top laminate layer. Bit should not cut into vertical edge surface.

16 File all edges smooth. Use downward file strokes to avoid chipping the laminate.

17 Cut 1¼"-wide strips of ¼" plywood to form over-hanging scribing strip for backsplash. Attach to top and sides of backsplash core with glue and wallboard screws. Cut laminate pieces and apply to exposed sides, top, and front of backsplash. Trim each piece as it is applied.

18 Test-fit countertop and backsplash. Because walls may be uneven, use compass to trace wall outline onto backsplash scribing strip. Use a belt sander to grind backsplash to scribe line (page124).

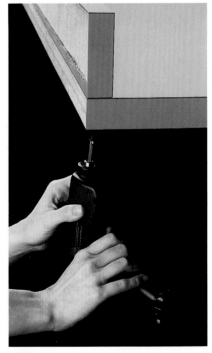

19 Apply bead of silicone caulk to the bottom edge of the backsplash.

20 Position the backsplash on the countertop, and clamp it into place with bar clamps. Wipe away excess caulk, and let dry completely.

21 Screw 2" wallboard screws through countertop into backsplash core. Make sure screwheads are countersunk completely for a tight fit against the base cabinet.

(continued next page)

Building a Ceramic Tile Countertop

Modern adhesives make it easy for a homeowner to install ceramic tile on a kitchen countertop and backsplash. Because kitchen surfaces are exposed to water, use moisture-resistant adhesive and glazed tiles. Tiles may be sold individually or in mosaic sheets attached to mesh backing. Some tiles have edge lugs that automatically set the width of grout joints. For smooth-edged tiles, use plastic spacers to maintain even grout joints.

A successful tile job requires a solid, flat base and careful planning. Dry-fit the tile job to make sure the finished layout is pleasing to the eye. After installation, seal the tile and grout with a quality silicone sealer to prevent water damage. Clean and reseal the tile periodically to maintain a new appearance.

Everything You Need:

Basic Hand Tools: tape measure, pencil, putty knife, framing square, caulk gun, hammer.

Basic Power Tools: circular saw, cordless screwdriver, orbital sander.

Basic Materials: ceramic tile, ¾" exterior (CDX) plywood, wood strips.

Specialty Tools & Materials: photo, page 136.

Ceramic tiles are available individually, or connected with mesh backing to form mosaic sheets. Ask your dealer to recommend tiles that will stand up to heavy countertop use.

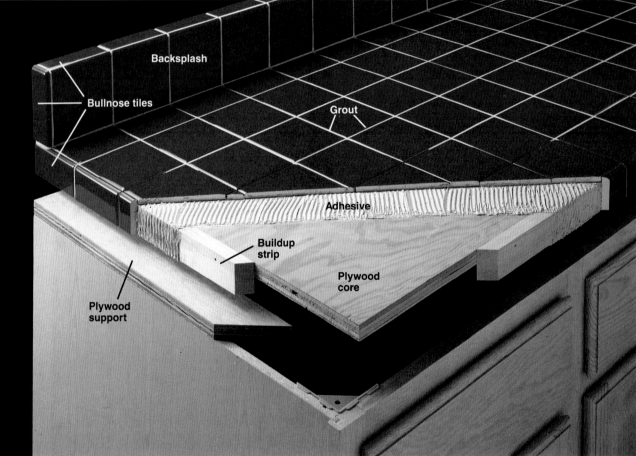

Backsplash

Bullnose tiles

Grout

Adhesive

Buildup strip

Plywood core

Plywood support

Ceramic tile countertop: Countertop core is ¾" exterior plywood cut to the same size as cabinet. Edges are built up with wood strips attached to outer edges of core. Tiles are set into place with adhesive. Grout fills gaps between tiles. Bullnose tiles, which have rounded edges, are used to cover edges of countertop and backsplash. Backsplash tiles can be installed over a separate plywood core, or directly to wall behind countertop. ¾" × 3" plywood supports are attached every 2 feet across base cabinet and around edges of cabinet.

Specialty tools & supplies include: sandpaper (A), denatured alcohol (B), latex grout additive (C), grout (D), silicone caulk (E), silicone sealer (F), carpenter's glue (G), latex underlayment (H), tile adhesive (I), short 2 × 4 wrapped in scrap carpeting (J), tile cutter (K), plastic spacers (L), foam paint brush (M), mallet (N), finish nails (O), wallboard screws (P), tile sander (Q), tile nippers (R), notched trowel (S), grout float (T), scoring tool (U).

How to Build a Ceramic Tile Countertop

Frame support

1 Cut 3" wide frame supports from ¾" exterior plywood. Use 1¼" wallboard screws or 4d common nails to attach supports every 24" across cabinet, around perimeter, and next to cutout locations. From ¾" exterior plywood, cut core to same size as cabinet unit (A × B), using a circular saw.

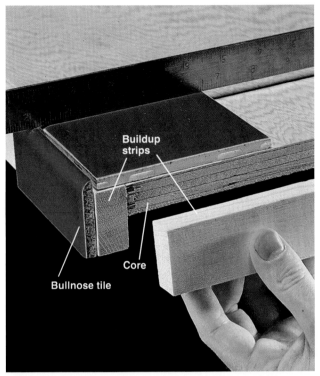

2 If countertop will have bullnose edge tiles, attach 1 × 2 buildup strips of pine or exterior plywood to exposed edges of countertop core, using carpenter's glue and 6d finish nails. Top of strip should be flush with top of core.

Option: for decorative wood edge, attach stained and sealed 1 × 2 hardwood strips to edge of core with carpenter's glue and finish nails. Top of edge strip should be flush with top surface of tile.

3 Position countertop core on cabinets and attach with sheetmetal or wallboard screws driven up through corner brackets inside cabinets. Screws should not be long enough to puncture top surface of core.

4 Use latex underlayment to fill any low spots and cracks in countertop core. Let underlayment dry, then sand smooth.

(continued next page)

5 To create a symmetrical tile layout, measure and mark the middle of the countertop core. Use a framing square to draw a layout line (A), perpendicular to the front edge of the core. Measure along line A from the front edge a distance equal to one full tile, and mark. Use the framing square to draw a second layout line (B) perpendicular to line A.

6 Dry-fit rows of tiles along layout lines. Use plastic spacers if tiles do not have self-spacing lugs. If dry-fit shows that layout is not pleasing, line A may be adjusted in either direction. Dry-fit all tiles, and mark cutting lines on any tiles that must be trimmed.

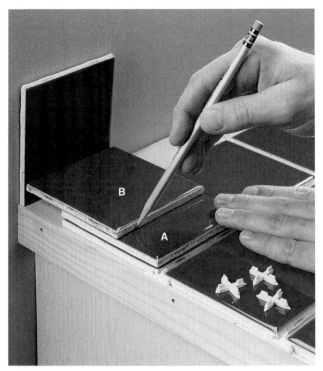

7 Mark border tiles for cutting. To allow for grout, place a tile upright against wall. Place a loose tile (A) over the last full tile. Place another tile (B) against upright tile, over tile A. Mark tile A and cut to fit border space.

8 To make straight cuts, place tile faceup in tile cutter. Adjust tool to proper width, then score a continuous line by pulling the cutting wheel firmly across face of tile.

9 Snap tile along scored line, as directed by tool manufacturer. Smooth the cut edges of tile with a tile sander.

10 For curved cuts, score a crosshatch outline of the cut with tile scoring tool. Use tile nippers to gradually break away small portions of tile until cutout is complete.

(continued next page)

11 Begin installation with edge tiles. Apply a thin layer of adhesive to edge of countertop and back of tile, using a notched trowel. Press tiles into place with a slight twist. Insert plastic spacers between tiles. (Self-spacing tiles require no plastic spacers.)

12 Remove dry-fit tiles next to layout lines. Spread adhesive along layout lines and install perpendicular rows of tiles. Use plastic spacers to maintain even spacing. Check alignment with framing square.

13 Install remaining tiles, working from layout line outward to ends. Work in small areas, about 18" square. Use denatured alcohol to remove any adhesive from face of tiles before it dries. For the backsplash, install a single row of bullnose tiles directly to wall, or build a separate backsplash core from ¾" plywood.

14 After each small area is installed, "set" the tiles. Wrap a short piece of 2 × 4 in scrap carpeting or a towel. Lay block against the tiles and tap lightly with a mallet or hammer. Remove plastic spacers with a toothpick.

15 Mix grout and latex additive. Apply grout with a rubber grout float. Use a sweeping motion to force grout into joints. Wipe away excess grout with a damp sponge. Let grout dry for 1 hour, then wipe away powdery haze. Let grout cure as directed by manufacturer before caulking and sealing.

16 Seal joints around backsplash with silicone caulk. Smooth bead with a wet finger. Wipe away excess caulk. Let caulk dry completely. Apply silicone sealer to countertop with a foam brush. Let dry, then apply second coat. Let dry, and buff with soft cloth.

Edge treatments include rounded bullnose tiles (top) cut to fit edge, and hardwood edge (bottom) shaped with a router. Hardwood edges should be attached and finished before tile is installed. Protect hardwood with masking tape when grouting and sealing the tile job.

Fixtures & Appliances

Make final connections for faucets, drains, and appliances after an electrician or plumber has finished the rough work. A licensed plumber or electrician will make sure the job conforms to local Codes.

Where Codes allow, have the electrician install plug-in outlets for all the major appliances. This makes it easy to disconnect the appliances for servicing.

If a remodeling job requires new plumbing and wiring, the work should be completed in the early stage of the project, before new flooring, cabinets, or appliances are installed.

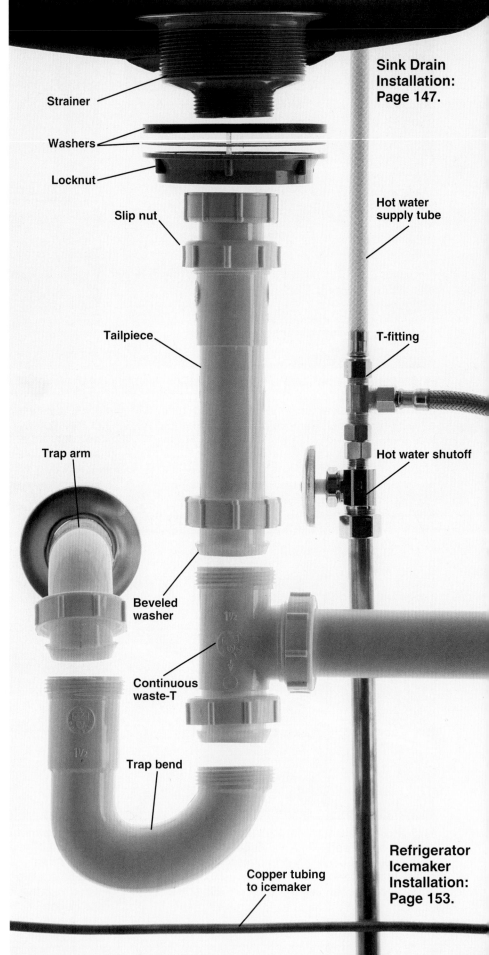

Sink Drain Installation: Page 147.

Strainer

Washers

Locknut

Slip nut

Hot water supply tube

Tailpiece

T-fitting

Hot water shutoff

Trap arm

Beveled washer

Continuous waste-T

Trap bend

Copper tubing to icemaker

Refrigerator Icemaker Installation: Page 153.

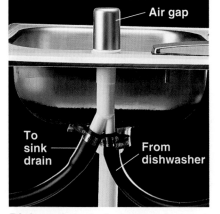

Air gap

To sink drain

From dishwasher

Dishwasher drain hose is looped up through an air gap device attached to the sink or countertop. Air gap is a safety feature that prevents a plugged sink drain from backing up into the dishwasher.

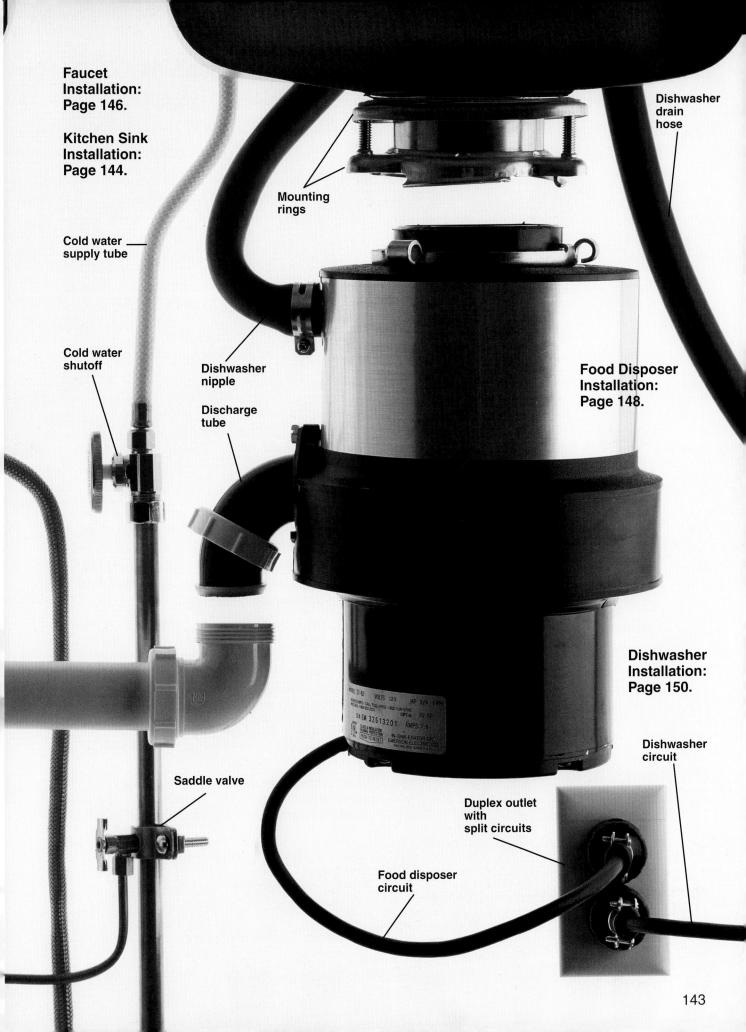

**Faucet
Installation:
Page 146.**

**Kitchen Sink
Installation:
Page 144.**

Cold water
supply tube

Mounting
rings

Cold water
shutoff

Dishwasher
drain
hose

Dishwasher
nipple

**Food Disposer
Installation:
Page 148.**

Discharge
tube

**Dishwasher
Installation:
Page 150.**

Saddle valve

Duplex outlet
with
split circuits

Dishwasher
circuit

Food disposer
circuit

143

Installing a Kitchen Sink

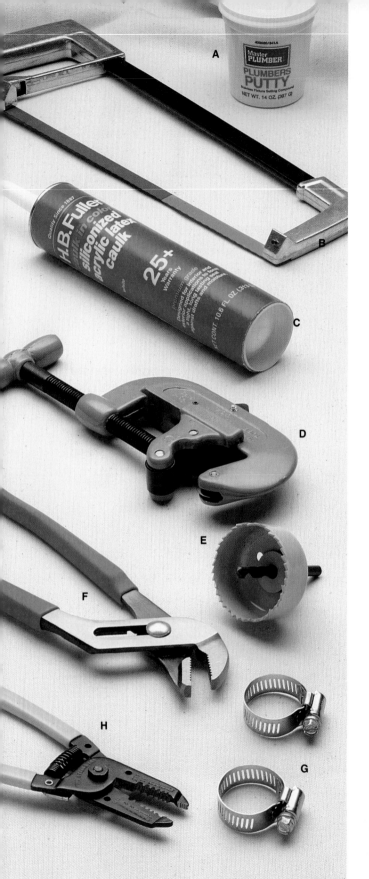

Kitchen sinks for do-it-yourself installation are made from cast iron coated with enamel, stainless steel, or enameled steel.

Cast-iron sinks are heavy, durable, and relatively easy to install. Most cast-iron sinks are frameless, requiring no mounting hardware.

Stainless steel and enameled steel sinks weigh less than cast iron. They may require a metal frame and mounting brackets. A good stainless steel sink is made of heavy 18- or 20-gauge nickel steel, which holds up well under use. Lighter steel (designated by numbers higher than 20) dents easily.

Some premium-quality sinks are made from solid-surface material or porcelain, and are usually installed by professionals.

When choosing a sink, make sure the predrilled openings will fit your faucet. To make the countertop cutout for a kitchen sink installation, see page 124.

Specialty Tools & Supplies for plumbing & appliance installation include: plumber's putty (A), hacksaw (B), silicone caulk (C), tubing cutter (D), hole saw (E), channel-type pliers (F), hose clamps (G), combination tool (H).

Everything You Need:

Basic Hand Tools: caulk gun, screwdriver.

Basic Materials: sink, sink frame, mounting clips.

Specialty Tools & Supplies: photo, left.

How to Install a Frameless Sink

1 After making countertop cutout, lay the sink upside down. Apply a ¼'' bead of silicone caulk or plumber's putty around the underside of sink flange.

2 Position front of sink in countertop cutout, by holding it from the drain openings. Carefully lower the sink into position. Press down to create a tight seal, then wipe away excess caulk.

How to Install a Framed Sink

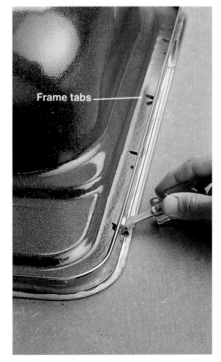

Frame tabs

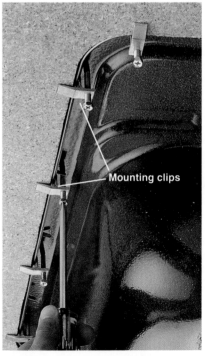

Mounting clips

1 Turn the sink frame upside down. Apply a ¼'' bead of silicone caulk or plumber's putty around both sides of the vertical flange.

2 Set the sink upside down inside the frame. Bend frame tabs to hold the sink. Carefully set the sink into the cutout opening, and press down to create a tight seal.

3 Hook mounting clips every 6'' to 8'' inches around the frame from underneath countertop. Tighten mounting screws. Wipe away excess caulk from the frame.

Installing a Faucet & Drain

Most new kitchen faucets feature single-handle control levers and washerless designs. They rarely require maintenance. More expensive designer styles offer added features, like colorful enameled finishes, detachable spray nozzles, or even digital temperature readouts.

Connect the faucet to hot and cold water lines with easy-to-install flexible supply tubes made from vinyl or braided steel.

Where local codes allow, use plastic piping for drain hookups. Plastic is inexpensive and easy to install.

A wide selection of extensions and angle fittings let you easily plumb any sink configuration. Manufacturers offer kits that contain all the fittings needed for attaching a food disposer or dishwasher to the sink drain system.

Everything You Need:

Basic Materials: faucet, flexible vinyl or braided steel supply tubes, drain components.

Specialty Tools & Supplies: photo, page 144.

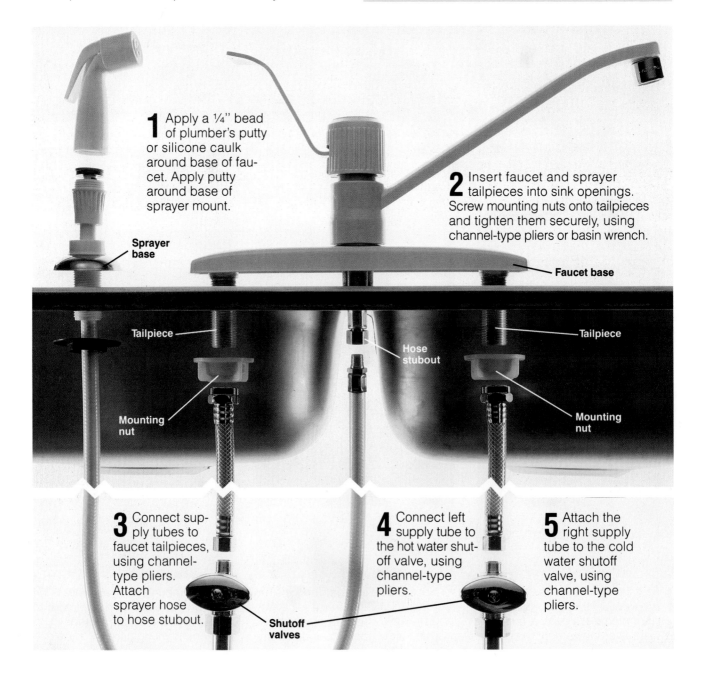

1 Apply a ¼" bead of plumber's putty or silicone caulk around base of faucet. Apply putty around base of sprayer mount.

Sprayer base

2 Insert faucet and sprayer tailpieces into sink openings. Screw mounting nuts onto tailpieces and tighten them securely, using channel-type pliers or basin wrench.

Faucet base

Tailpiece

Hose stubout

Tailpiece

Mounting nut

Mounting nut

3 Connect supply tubes to faucet tailpieces, using channel-type pliers. Attach sprayer hose to hose stubout.

Shutoff valves

4 Connect left supply tube to the hot water shut-off valve, using channel-type pliers.

5 Attach the right supply tube to the cold water shutoff valve, using channel-type pliers.

How to Attach Drain Lines

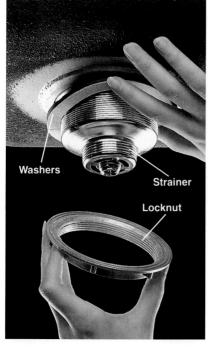

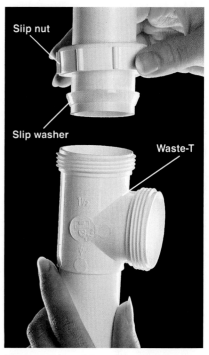

1 Install sink strainer in each sink drain opening. Apply ¼'' bead of plumber's putty around bottom of flange. Insert strainer into drain opening. Place rubber and fiber washers over neck of strainer. Screw locknut onto neck and tighten with channel-type pliers.

2 Attach tailpiece to strainer. Place insert washer in flared end of tailpiece, then attach tailpiece by screwing a slip nut onto sink strainer. If necessary, tailpiece can be cut to fit with a hacksaw.

3 On sinks with two basins, use a continuous waste-T-fitting to join the tailpieces (pages 142 to 143). Attach the fitting with slip washers and nuts. Beveled side of washers faces threaded portion of pipes.

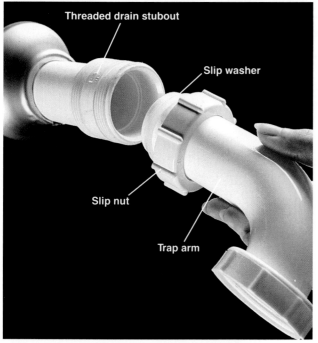

4 Attach the trap arm to the drain stubout, using a slip nut and washer. Beveled side of washer should face threaded drain stubout. If necessary, trap arm can be cut to fit with a hacksaw.

5 Attach trap bend to trap arm, using slip nuts and washers. Beveled side of washers should face trap bend. Tighten all nuts with channel-type pliers.

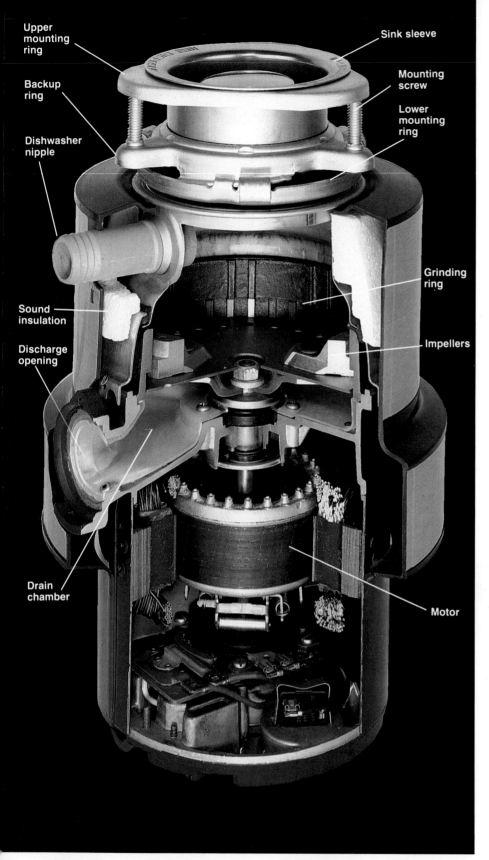

Upper mounting ring

Backup ring

Dishwasher nipple

Sound insulation

Discharge opening

Drain chamber

Sink sleeve

Mounting screw

Lower mounting ring

Grinding ring

Impellers

Motor

Food disposer grinds food waste so it can be flushed away through the sink drain system. A quality disposer has a ½-horsepower, self-reversing motor that will not jam. Other features to look for include foam sound insulation, a cast-iron grinding ring, and overload protection that allows the motor to be reset if it overheats. Better food disposers have a 5-year manufacturer's warranty.

Installing a Food Disposer

Choose a food disposer with a motor rated at ½ horsepower or more. Look for a self-reversing feature that prevents the disposer from jamming. Better models carry a manufacturer's warranty of up to five years.

Local plumbing codes may require that a disposer be plugged into a grounded outlet controlled by a switch above the sink.

Everything You Need:

Basic Hand Tools: screwdriver.

Basic Materials: 12-gauge appliance cord with grounded plug, wire nuts.

Specialty Tools & Supplies: photo, page 144.

How to Install a Food Disposer

1 Remove plate on bottom of disposer. Use combination tool to strip about ½" of insulation from each wire in appliance cord. Connect white wires, using a wire nut. Connect black wires. Attach green insulated wire to green ground screw. Gently push wires into opening. Replace bottom plate.

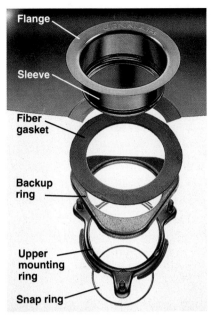

2 Apply ¼-inch bead of plumber's putty under the flange of the disposer sink sleeve. Insert sleeve in drain opening, and slip the fiber gasket and the backup ring onto the sleeve. Place upper mounting ring on sleeve and slide snap ring into groove.

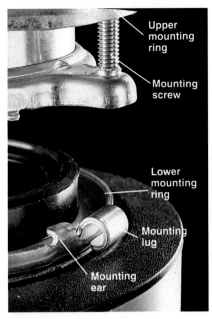

3 Tighten the three mounting screws. Hold disposer against upper mounting ring so that the mounting lugs on the lower mounting ring are directly under the mounting screws. Turn the lower mounting ring clockwise until the disposer is supported by the mounting assembly.

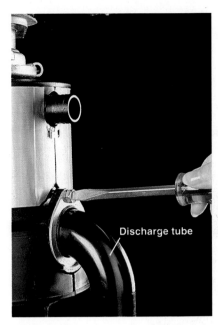

4 Attach the discharge tube to the discharge opening on the side of the disposer, using the rubber washer and metal flange.

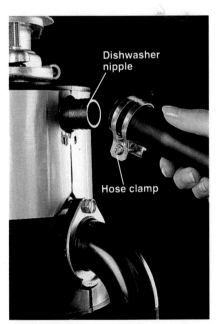

5 If dishwasher will be attached, knock out the plug in the dishwasher nipple, using a screwdriver. Attach the dishwasher drain hose to nipple with hose clamp.

6 Attach the discharge tube to continuous waste pipe with slip washer and nut. If discharge tube is too long, cut it with a hacksaw or tubing cutter.

7 Lock disposer into place. Insert a screwdriver or disposer wrench into a mounting lug on the lower mounting ring, and turn clockwise until the mounting ears are locked. Tighten all drain slip nuts with channel-type pliers.

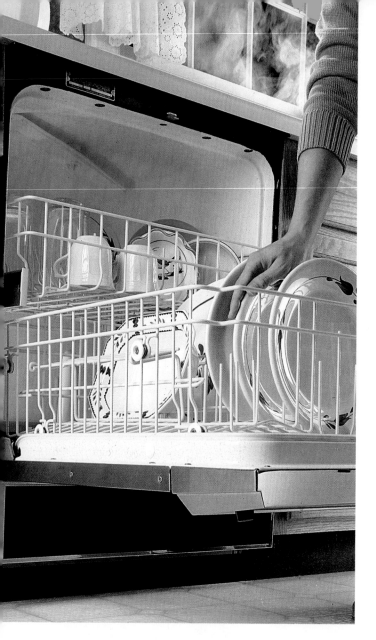

Installing a Dishwasher

A dishwasher requires a hot water supply connection, a drain connection, and an electrical hookup. These connections are easiest to make when the dishwasher is located next to the sink.

Hot water reaches the dishwasher through a supply tube. With a multiple-outlet shutoff valve or brass T-fitting on the hot water pipe, you can control water to the sink and dishwasher with the same valve.

For safety, loop the dishwasher drain hose up through an air gap mounted on the sink or countertop. An air gap prevents a clogged drain from backing up into the dishwasher.

A dishwasher requires its own 20-amp electrical circuit. For convenience, have this circuit wired into one-half of a split duplex receptacle. The other half of the receptacle powers the food disposer.

Everything You Need:

Basic Hand Tools: screwdriver, utility knife.

Basic Power Tools: drill with 2" hole saw.

Basic Materials: air gap, drain hose, waste-T tailpiece, braided steel supply tube, rubber connector for food disposer, brass L-fitting, 12-gauge appliance power cord.

Specialty Tools & Supplies: photo, page 144.

How to Install a Dishwasher

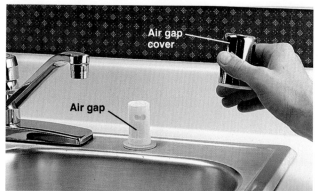

1 Mount air gap, using one of the predrilled sink openings. Or, bore a hole in the countertop with a drill and hole saw. Attach the air gap by tightening mounting nut over the tailpiece with channel-type pliers.

2 Cut openings in side of sink base cabinet for electrical and plumbing lines, using a drill and hole saw. Dishwasher instructions specify size and location of openings. Slide dishwasher into place, feeding rubber drain hose through hole in cabinet. Level the dishwasher.

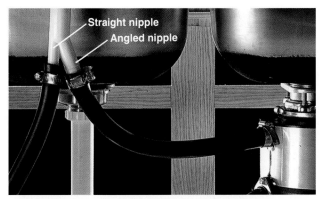

3 Attach the dishwasher drain hose to the smaller, straight nipple on the air gap, using a hose clamp. If hose is too long, cut to correct length with a utility knife. Cut another length of rubber hose to reach from the larger, angled nipple to the food disposer. Attach hose to the air gap and to the nipple on disposer with hose clamps.

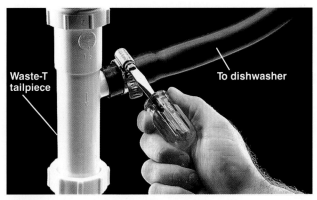

On sinks without food disposer, attach a special waste-T sink tailpiece to sink strainer. Attach the drain hose to the waste-T nipple with a hose clamp.

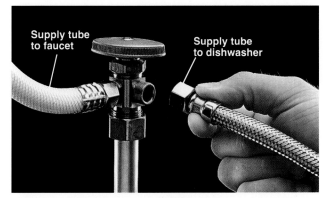

4 Connect dishwasher supply tube to hot water shut-off, using channel-type pliers. This connection is easiest with a multiple-outlet shutoff valve or a brass T-fitting (page 142).

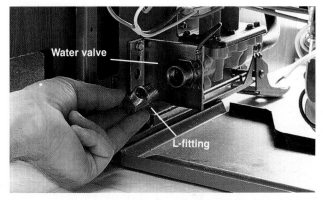

5 Remove access panel on front of dishwasher. Connect a brass L-fitting to the threaded opening on the dishwasher water valve, and tighten with channel-type pliers.

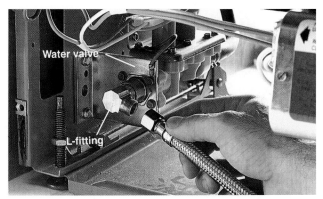

6 Run the braided steel supply tube from the hot water pipe to the dishwasher water valve. Attach supply tube to L-fitting, using channel-type pliers.

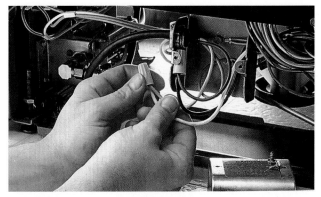

7 Remove cover on electrical box. Run power cord from outlet through to electrical box. Strip about ½" of insulation from each cord wire, using combination tool. Connect black wires, using a wire nut. Connect white wires. Connect green insulated wire to ground screw. Replace box cover and dishwasher access panel.

Installing Appliances & Water Filtration Systems

New appliances may require updated or new wiring, plumbing or gas lines. Large electrical appliances each require a separate circuit. Gas lines should have accessible shutoff valves, and should be installed by a professional.

Water filtration systems are available for the whole house and for point of use. Whole-house systems are effective for reducing amounts of sediment and chlorine. Point-of-use systems are very effective at reducing lead and bacteria. Installing both provides the best-tasting and safest water.

Everything You Need:

Basic Hand Tools: plumbing tools.
Basic Materials: ¼" soft copper tubing, saddle valves, brass compression fittings.

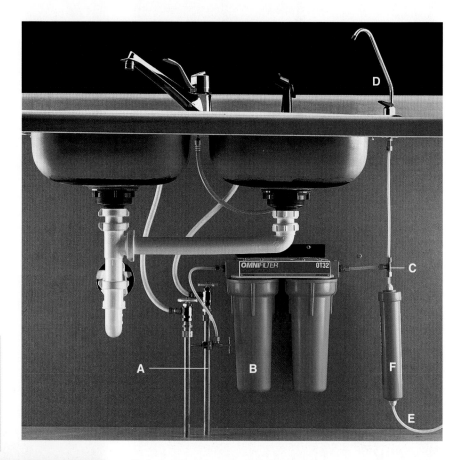

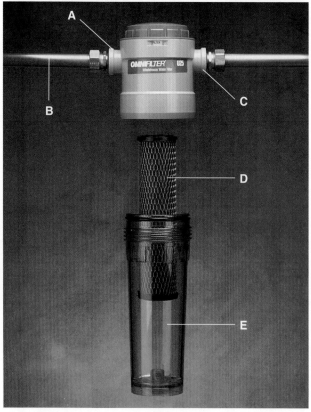

Point-of-use water filtration system (above) is easily installed underneath the kitchen sink, and other sinks where potable water is used. Attach a saddle valve (A) to the cold water supply pipe (see opposite page). Tubing connects the intake side of the filtration unit (B) to the saddle valve. Tubing connects the outtake side of the filtration unit to a T-valve (C). Additional tubing connects this valve to the faucet (D) and to the refrigerator/ice-maker line (E). Another filter (F) can be installed in the tubing for the refrigerator/ice maker for additional protection. See below for filter replacement information.

Whole-house filtration system (shown in exploded view, left) is installed in the pipe carrying water to the house from the water meter. The intake side of the filtration unit (A) is connected to the pipe to the water meter (B). Pipe supplying filtered water to the house is connected to the outtake side of the unit (C). Filters (D) must be replaced every few months, depending on type and manufacturer. The filtration unit cover (E) unscrews for filter access.

How to Connect Refrigerator Icemaker

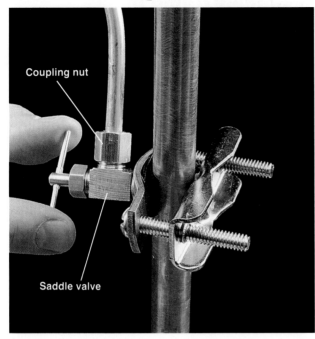

1 Shut off water at main shutoff valve. Attach a ¼" saddle valve to cold water pipe. Connect ¼" soft copper tubing to saddle valve with compression ring and coupling nut. Closing spigot fully causes spike inside valve to puncture water pipe.

2 Run copper tubing to refrigerator. Connect water supply tube to the water valve tube, using a ¼" compression elbow. Slide coupling nuts and compression rings over tubes, and insert tubes into elbow. Tighten coupling nuts with channel-type pliers.

How to Make Electrical Connections

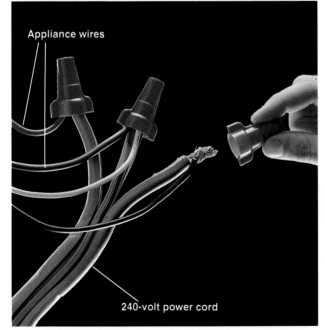

Use wire nuts to connect power cord to appliance wires. Power cord for a 240-volt appliance has three leads. Turn power off. Strip about ⅝" of insulation from each lead. Attach the white appliance wire, and green wire (if present), to the middle lead on power cord, using a large wire nut. Attach red and black appliance wires to the outside leads on power cord.

How to Connect Gas Lines

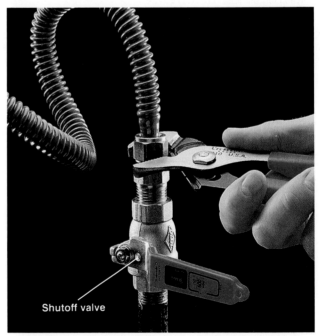

Connect flexible gas tubing to shutoff valve and to appliance, using channel-type pliers. Follow local code requirements for gas connections.

153

Installing a Vent Hood

A vent hood eliminates heat, moisture, and cooking vapors from your kitchen. It has an electric fan unit with one or more filters, and a system of metal ducts to vent air to the outdoors. A ducted vent hood is more efficient than a ductless model, which filters and recirculates air without removing it.

Metal ducts for a vent hood can be round or rectangular. Elbows and transition fittings are available for both types of ducts. These fittings let you vent around corners, or join duct components that differ in shape or size.

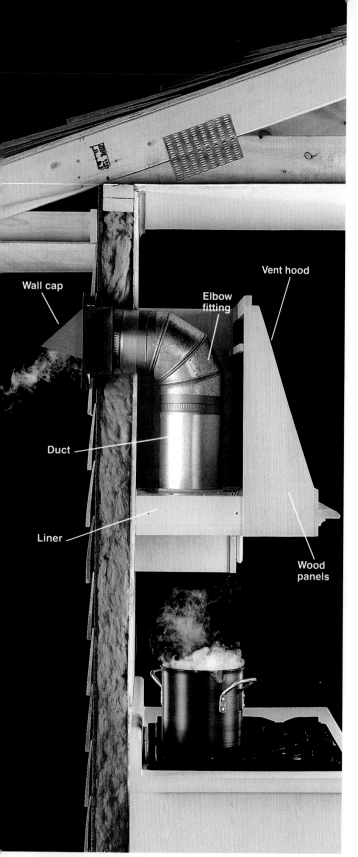

Wall-mounted vent hood (shown in cutaway) is installed between wall cabinets. Fan unit is fastened to a metal liner that is anchored to cabinets. Duct and elbow fitting exhaust cooking vapors to the outdoors through a wall cap. Vent fan and duct are covered by wood or laminate panels that match cabinet finish.

Labels on cutaway photo: Wall cap, Duct, Liner, Elbow fitting, Vent hood, Wood panels.

Specialty tools & supplies include: reciprocating saw with coarse wood-cutting blade (A), silicone caulk (B), duct tape (C), wire nuts (D), ⅛" twist bit (E), No. 9 counterbore drill bit (F), ¾" sheetmetal screws (G), 2½" sheetmetal screws (H), combination tool (I), masonry chisel (J), 2" masonry nails (K), metal snips (L), masonry drill bit (M), ball peen hammer (N).

How to Install a Wall-mounted Vent Hood

1 Attach ¾" × 4" × 12" wooden cleats to sides of the cabinets with 1¼" wallboard screws. Follow manufacturer's directions for proper distance from cooking surface.

2 Position the hood liner between the cleats and attach with ¾" sheetmetal screws.

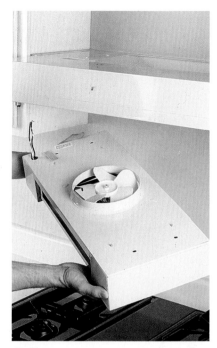

3 Remove cover panels for light, fan, and electrical compartments on fan unit, as directed by manufacturer. Position fan unit inside liner and fasten by attaching nuts to mounting bolts inside light compartments.

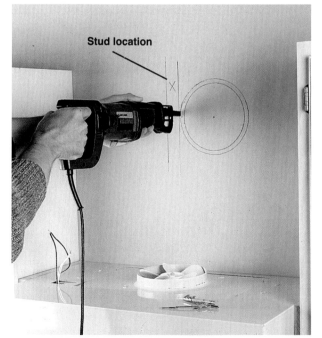

4 Locate studs in wall where duct will pass, using a stud finder. Mark hole location. Hole should be ½" larger that diameter of duct. Complete cutout with a reciprocating saw or jig saw. Remove any wall insulation. Drill a pilot hole through outside wall.

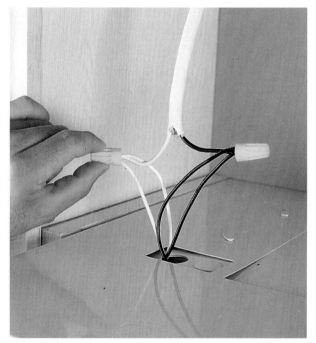

5 Strip about ½" of plastic insulation from each wire in the circuit cable, using combination tool. Connect the black wires, using a wire nut. Connect the white wires. Gently push the wires into the electrical box. Replace the coverpanels on the light and fan compartments.

(continued next page)

6 Make duct cutout on exterior wall. On masonry, drill a series of holes around outline of cutout. Remove waste with a masonry chisel and ball peen hammer. On wood siding, make cutout with a reciprocating saw.

7 Attach first duct section by sliding the smooth end over the outlet flange on the vent hood. Cut duct sections to length with metal snips.

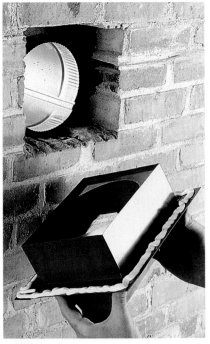

8 Drill three or four pilot holes around joint through both layers of metal, using ⅛" twist bit. Attach duct with ¾" sheetmetal screws. Seal joint with duct tape.

9 Join additional duct sections by sliding smooth end over corrugated end of preceding section. Use an adjustable elbow to change directions in duct run. Secure all joints with sheetmetal screws and duct tape.

10 Install duct cap on exterior wall. Apply a thick bead of silicone caulk to cap flange. Slide cap over end of duct.

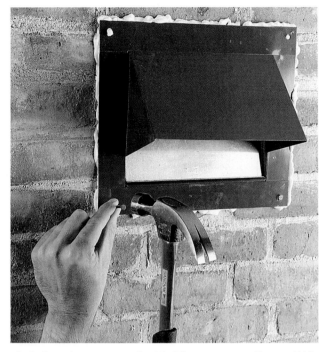

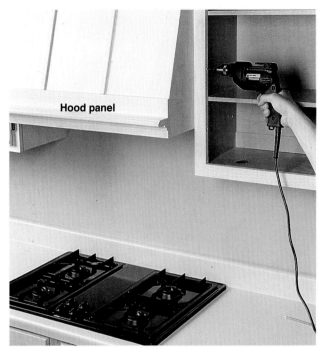

11 Attach cap to wall with 2" masonry nails, or 1½" sheetmetal screws (on wood siding). Wipe away excess caulk.

12 Slide the decorative hood panel into place between the wall cabinets. Drill pilot holes through the cabinet face frame with a counterbore bit. Attach the hood panel to the cabinets with 2½" sheetmetal screws.

Vent Hood Variations

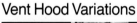

Downdraft cooktop has a built-in blower unit that vents through the back or the bottom of a base cabinet. A downdraft cooktop is a good choice for a kitchen island or peninsula.

Cabinet-mounted vent hood is attached to the bottom of a short, 12" to 18" tall wall cabinet. Metal ducts run inside this wall cabinet.

INDEX